Shoots out of Eden

Christian Monastic Gardening in the British Isles

By

Francis Beswick

Published 2007 by arima publishing

www.arimapublishing.com

ISBN 978-1-84549-220-5

© Francis Beswick 2007

All rights reserved

This book is copyright. Subject to statutory exception and to provisions of relevant collective licensing agreements, no part of this publication may be reproduced, stored in a retrieval system, or transmitted in any form or by any means, without the prior written permission of the author.

Printed and bound in the United Kingdom

Typeset in Palatino Linotype 11/16

This book is sold subject to the conditions that it shall not, by way of trade or otherwise, be lent, re-sold, hired out, or otherwise circulated without the publisher's prior consent in any form of binding or cover other than that which it is published and without a similar condition including this condition being imposed on the subsequent purchaser.

Abramis is an imprint of arima publishing

arima publishing
ASK House, Northgate Avenue
Bury St Edmunds, Suffolk IP32 6BB
t: (+44) 01284 700321

www.arimapublishing.com

This book is dedicated to my wife Maureen

In recognition of many years of loyalty

Preface

This book grew out of a study performed for the Horticultural Correspondence College, through which I studied Horticulture. When they proposed that I write a project to accompany my advanced certificate I decided that I would combine my three great interests, Religion, History and Horticulture. A study of Christian monastic gardens fitted the criteria exactly. I decided to restrict the scope of the study to the British Isles, both Britain and Ireland, because of the limitations of time that a research project suffers. I must confess to a love of the British Isles. They are my home, the place whose history I have studied and the place where I wish to live out my life. However, much of the study is not specific to Britain, because British and Irish monasteries were part of a universal church and therefore drew on traditions that transcended mere national identity and boundaries. It was only when I came to a chronological account of monastic gardens that I focused on Britain and Ireland.

There are people whom I must thank for their help. From the Horticultural Correspondence College Oliver Menhinnick, the senior tutor, and Michael Farr, my tutor and project supervisor, both richly deserve to be thanked. Felix Gorton, my first tutor, must not be omitted from the list of people to whom thanks are owed, for he began the tutorial process that led me to my first certificate and ultimately this work. Andrew Beswick, my eldest son, a nurseryman and artist, who shares my passion for religion and horticulture, produced some artwork for me. I must thank the St Lawrence Trust at South Walsham for their kindness in sending me information to help with the research.

The year is 1588. Armada beacons are blazing and the young men are hot for war. As evening approaches an old man steals silently into an abbey already crumbling into ruins. He notes sadly that looters have taken more stones from the walls, and that even more of the roof has fallen. The church where he once worshipped is now too unsafe to enter. His mind wanders back to the year 1539 when he and his brethren were expelled and the property sold to fund the king's wars and luxury lifestyle. He is deeply resentful but totally impotent to right the deeply felt wrong. Quietly he goes into what was once the paradise garden adjoining the church. Some of the shrubs that he planted are still forcing their way through the riot of nettles, bindweed and thistle that have claimed the once cultivated land. He surreptitiously clears a small patch, as he always does when he has the opportunity; he tends the burial garden in honour of his departed brethren; and then the one-time monastery gardener hurries away, lest he be taken as a traitor at this sensitive time. In the quiet of the loft above the farmhouse where he now lives and works he remembers how things once were, when the gardens were rich in flowers, fruit and vegetables. An old man, he has never married, for he is faithful to the vows that he swore when times were favourable to his kind. He was not one of the monks who took a state pension, because he did not swear the oath of allegiance to accept Henry the Eighth as head of the church of England, and has not done so to any of Henry's successors. The monk has opted not to go abroad, for he is too rooted in England to move to another land, and anyway he speaks no French or Spanish. He repeats the divine office, quietly in Latin, the use of which would be deemed evidence of treasonous intent, and then wrapping himself in his blanket he settles beside the chimneystack to catch some of the warmth of the fire rising from below and seeks the peace that comes in slumber. His employer knows who he is, what he once was and what he still does, but like most English people he has less taste for persecution than the government does. So the old man is left alone.

Meanwhile in Scotland a few monks linger in the ruins of Melrose. They are old men, all of them, for the monastery is nearly derelict as the result of war and persecution. They still continue with their way of life, but their numbers dwindle yearly, the graveyard is fuller year by year and the inward flow of novices has ceased; and they are deeply impoverished. Occasionally people from the North of England pass by and stop in for mass, giving a welcome donation. The monks still till the vegetable garden, but they find that the digging becomes harder as they age. Soon there will be none and the monastery will be left to crumble sadly into silence.

Scenes like this are never recorded in the history books, which mainly speak of a few great men and even fewer women. But they must have occurred. For many years after the dissolution of the monasteries there lived in Britain a large number of one-time monks and nuns. Some took up employment in the Church of England; some went to monasteries abroad; others faded into lay life, with the nuns in particular finding the security that could only come to a woman of that time from marriage; but there would have been a few like the imaginary monks above, trying to hang on to what was left of their old lives, who lingered long hoping for the return of better times. The last probably died in the early sixteen hundreds and his grave is forgotten.

The pain must have been great for monastery gardeners. Gardeners become attached to their gardens, because something of themselves goes into the land that they till, and monastery gardeners were no exception to this. But their gardens were more than ordinary gardens. They were spiritual places, parts of a spiritual enclave, in which the garden was a consecrated place, integral to a unique spiritual way of life, and this made the pain of loss all the greater. The history books discuss the dissolution of the monasteries in political and economic terms, dispassionately [supposedly] weighing up benefits and losses and assessing causes and effects, but they rarely record the pain of the small people whose lives were torn apart. Those books which deal with the effects on the ordinary people can never capture the names of many individuals or tell their stories, for they are unrecorded. Consequences are measured on a public scale, but their impact on individual human feelings is overlooked, especially because it is mostly unrecorded. But it is on the impact of change on small, ordinary lives that political, economic and religious change must be measured because politics exists for the unimportant, ordinary folk, not just for the great and powerful. The monk above is imaginary, but he is representative of the anonymous many of his kind.

So what was it that inspired the monk-gardeners as they toiled and tilled? How did they understand their work and its meaning? We cannot ask them, for they left few records other than accounts, and most wrote nothing of their work. But we can examine the religious culture to which they belonged to seek for an insight into their thoughts, feelings and purposes.

Christian thought on gardens.

Religion has inspired the design and planting of gardens throughout the ages. This is not surprising, for religion contains humanity's deepest longings and most enduring values, and thus has found expression in art and architecture. As gardening is landscape architecture, the religious principles that inspire people to create religious architecture will inspire them to create gardens. Different religions, as we might expect, have their own characteristic gardening models, reflecting their specific beliefs and values, there being Islamic, Taoist, Buddhist gardens, etc. Christianity is particularly rich in garden design, and one broad type of Christian garden is the monastic garden, which expresses the values characteristic of the monastic way of life.

A Christian garden is a microcosm of the Christian world because those who design and tend it are inspired by Christian beliefs and values. According to Palmer, Christian gardens are characterised by beauty and utility [1]. The beauty is a means by which humans give glory to God, and so creating and tending a garden is therefore an act of prayer. For a person who is truly imbued with the Christian spirit it is the offering made by a lover, man, to a loved one, God, part of the ongoing dialogue between God and man. It is beautifying God's sanctuary, the world, the place that was his temple long before humans thought of building elaborate temples and churches.

In fact, to mediaeval thinkers nature was not only a temple, but also a classroom. In mediaeval Christian thought there were two "books" by which God was revealed: the book of Scripture and the book of nature.

Scripture obviously is the Bible; but nature is the world, be it the wild or the cultivated. Together the two books spoke of God, revealing him to his people. In nature humans see God at work; they contemplate his wonders and the glories that he has created, and thus they come to know him. Nature, however, should not be identified solely with wildness untouched by humankind. A well-tended garden could reveal God as much as a wilderness or a glorious natural scene could. After all, a garden was an image of Eden, an attempt to recapture the world as it was before sin entered it. For a Benedictine monk a well-tended garden was the sort of environment in which the divine was revealed, in its order, which revealed God's governing power, and its gentleness and civility, which reflected the Christian spirit that he wanted to imbue into his people. But we must not think that the monk regarded the book of nature as a source to be studied in a merely academic way. Like Scripture nature was to be approached in faith and an earnest desire to find God. It was to be approached in a meditative, reflective way. The mere possession of knowledge of God is not what monasticism is about. It is a loving-knowledge that comes from dialogue between a lover and his beloved. This supplements rather than excludes the practical knowledge that is involved in gardening. The monk could be reflecting whilst gardening.

While there is no absolute rule on the matter, an institution run on the principle that God is known through nature and Scripture would therefore expect to provide opportunities to experience both. Furthermore, to provide a humane, aesthetically pleasing and spiritual life for the monks and nuns, there must be some greenery and opportunities to interact with nature, either as a worker or as an enjoyer, or both. If people are to live and work in an institution, it must be conducive to a civilised, dignified and satisfying life.

But besides all that has been said above, monasteries are places particularly suited to gardening, for they are stable institutions that have often remained on the same site for hundreds of years, leaving time for gardens to develop and be honed to a high standard of horticultural perfection. Furthermore, the monastic way of life is conducive to skilful horticulture, for the monk's values of diligence and patience are what make gardeners efficient and make gardens thrive. The monk who can find the eternal in a flower and see spiritual significance in even the tiniest of actions is not likely to neglect his garden out of boredom. The Christian and therefore the monastic ideal is that the love that is cultivated in prayer spills over into the cultivation of the garden and returns to God as an offering of beautiful and useful plants, making "Something beautiful for God" as Mother Teresa was wont to say.

For Christians work of whatever kind, be it professional or menial, is an act that confers dignity upon the doer, who shares in the creative role of God. Thus a gardener shares in the divine role of creation, tending the Earth to make it more beautiful and productive. The old myth of Adam as the gardener of Eden reveals the Christian ideal, humans working in harmony with God in a beautiful and well-tended world, caring for the Earth under God's benign lordship. In this state of primal innocence work is a pleasure rather than a burden. In a sense every Christian garden is a celebration of Eden, the world as it ought to have been before humanity wrought its damage. The story of Adam and Eve is myth rather than historical fact, but it contains several great truths. One is that as evil entered the world, humans lost their harmony with creation and the environment became less friendly to humanity. Another overlooked point in the story was that Eve was as much a gardener as Adam, for the command to care for the Earth was given equally to both. In the modern age when human greed is ravaging the planet, global temperatures rise to dangerous levels, and sea levels rise, the myth of Eden expresses an important, eternal truth that humans can only live in a healthy and nurturing environment if they live in an ethically responsible way, rejecting materialism in favour of more spiritual living.

Christian monks are obliged to work for their living. Unlike Buddhist monks, who ideally live by begging [at least in Buddhist countries], Christian monks must earn their keep. Thus monks often worked in the monastery garden, the farm or at other economic and socially useful activities undertaken by the monastery. In Christianity and therefore monasteries manual work is regarded with as much respect as "professional" work, for all kinds of work are means of serving God and bettering society and the earth.

As all Christian life is to be lived in the love of God, in planting and tending a beautiful garden, Christian monks keep the first commandment, which is to love God. Gardening is praying with the hands. The garden is an inspiration for prayer and a place congenial to it. For Rhabanus Maurus the garden was a metaphor for the Christian Church, in which the various plants symbolically reflected the fruits of the Holy Spirit [2.] Rhabanus liked to have biblical plants in his monastic garden, plants that are mentioned in Scripture, such as lily of the valley and rose of Sharon, and so his garden was an artistic expression of his biblical studies, with each plant known for its religious significance. Some forms of Christian meditation use physical objects as a stimulus. The beauty of the garden may well be in inspiration to those who want to dwell on the goodness and glory of the creator. Monks were supposed to enjoy the garden, but to see in it the ephemeral nature of life in this world and therefore to reflect on the One who is the source of goodness and beauty.

The second commandment is love your neighbour, so Christian gardens will serve humans, for they provide food, herbs for healing and emotional therapy for the distressed, both monks and others. They are thus places useful to humans.

In mediaeval Christian thought gardening was considered a high activity. High activities were those that expressed the noblest Christian values. They were the activities of the gentle soul, which could be offered to God. Hunting by contrast was seen as a low activity, necessary and therefore not sinful, but hardly the activity of gentle souls, so monks and priests were forbidden to hunt. Gardening not only expressed the gentle virtues of Christianity, but also nourished and fostered them, for we learn and grow by doing and participating. In tending the garden the monk-gardener tended his own soul. In gardening humans fulfil the original commandment given in Eden to be fruitful and till the Earth. It is important to note that the Biblical injunction to be masters of the earth is oft mistranslated to justify exploitation of nature. The correct translation for master is steward, one who manages and tends a place put into his care for a higher master. For monks stewardship of the earth was expressed in their care for their gardens and the lands they owned.

The power of Christian stewardship is shown in the work of the Benedictines. Palmer states that towards the end of the Roman empire the land of Europe was ecologically degraded by Roman latefundism, in which the agri-barons of the period bought up land and exploited it until it was degraded [3] The Benedictines began the process of ecological healing, carefully nursing the land in their possession back to health. Later on, the Cistercians sought out wild and poor land for their penitential lifestyle. It was due to their efforts that much land in Europe came under tillage. In fact, monks made an enormous contribution to the well-cultivated landscape of Europe. Without them Europe would not be the fertile land that it is.

Monastic Gardens

Christian gardens commenced with the origins of monasticism, although at the earliest stage their religious format was embryonic. Antony the Abbot, the first hermit, planted vines and dug a waterhole at his desert dwelling. Other hermits maintained small gardens for food. Even when monasticism proper developed under Pachomius, monastic gardens were just vegetable patches. It was only as monasticism became more organized that a specific monastic garden model began to be discerned.

At this point it is necessary to give a few definitions:
- Monks and enclosed nuns live in a settled community under a religious rule. Monastic communities tend to be well established on a site for a sustained period of time, often centuries. Benedictine monks take a vow of stability, which is to stay in the monastery in which they were originally professed as monks, unless there are pressing reasons to move.
- Friars. Like monks in many ways, but they are mendicant, which means that they move about in the world much more than monks do. Franciscans are the classic examples of Friars. Friaries have gardens, but they have no distinct gardening traditions that can be identified. Furthermore, the friars had their houses in towns so as to be nearer to the poor whom they served, so the sites of their gardens are almost always built over now.
- Regular canons: These were originally ordinary priests who were organised under a rule. They are much more active in the world outside the monastery than monks are. No specific

gardening tradition can be discerned among them. They almost certainly followed the monastic model outlined below. In this work I am concentrating on the monastic orders.

As monasticism developed there arose three major monastic traditions: the rules of Benedict, Basil and Columbanus. In the first few centuries there was a variety of traditions, but they tended to distil themselves into three broad rules. Since the time of Charlemagne the Benedictine rule has been the norm for Catholic monks, though the Orthodox Church uses the rule of St Basil. The Cistercian and Carthusian religious orders follow the Benedictine rule with specific adaptations, as do other monastic orders not mentioned in this work. The Celtic church maintained the rule of Columbanus until Roman domination spread the rule of St Benedict. Columbanus did not invent Celtic monasticism, it was far older than he, but he formulated the rule in writing. In gardening terms there was little or nothing to choose between the Benedictine rule and that of Basil, as they both drew on Mediterranean and Middle Eastern sources, though the Celtic monks drew on cultural traditions somewhat different from the rest of their church. The rule of Basil was not known in the British Isles until quite recently. It is important to note that everything said here applies to convents of nuns as well as monasteries.

The Celtic Monastic Tradition

Celtic monasticism is now extinct, crushed between the hammer of the Viking raids on Ireland's monasteries and the anvil of the papal policy of regulating all Catholic monastic life under the Benedictine rule. Papal policy was not brutal, but it pressed any Celtic monasteries on the continent to adopt the Benedictine rule, because the stability preferred by the Benedictine rule fitted well the church's policy of working towards a stable, safe and orderly society. The decline of Celtic monasticism accelerated when the Vikings ravaged Irish monasteries. Young Irishmen forced to go abroad to study went into Benedictine foundations, bringing home the Benedictine rule with them, and the Celtic tradition simply faded away. Little is known of Celtic monastic gardening, but as Ireland had no urban life and mainly pastoral traditions, no organized gardening tradition arose in that land. Certainly the Irish monks had vegetable gardens, but we know little of them other than from archaeology. The quintessential Celtic monastery was a collection of buildings without any formal structure, with land to till outside the walls and maybe small plots inside them. Irish monasteries as far as we know had no prescribed structure. Furthermore, Ireland produced not only monasteries large and small, but also many hermits, who dwelt in little huts in remote places. We can still find the hermits' cells, but all trace of their vegetable gardens has been obliterated by time.

Celtic Christianity always saw the presence of God in wilderness and in liminal places. These are places on the edge, where life is challenged, where land meets sea, the tops of mountains etc. Inspired by Egyptian monasticism, which probably brought Christianity to

Erin before Saint Patrick set foot on its shores, they inherited the Egyptian Fathers' love of the desert[a], they sought out lonely places to meet God in the light of the sun, the crash of waves, the songs of birds and deep silence. The love that Irish monks bore for the wilderness derives from not only the Desert Fathers [the name given to the earliest Christian hermits, fierce ascetics who dwelt in deserts and came into broader Christian society once a year for Easter communion] but also from the Bible, in which significant religious experiences occurred in deserts, for example, the Theophany of Sinai, Elijah's encounter with God on Mount Horeb and Jesus' temptations. In this Celtic tradition formal gardens are less significant than wilderness, and as far as we know they were not developed.

A Celtic monk's hut

---

[a] The Desert Fathers were the earliest Christian hermits who sought out wilderness places in the Egyptian desert so that they could pray undisturbed. Monasticism later developed when some of them found it important to band together for mutual support in health, economics and worship.

The Benedictines

The Benedictine order arose in the last days of the Western Roman Empire, beginning on the summit of Monte Casino. In the collapsing empire the first and foremost social priority was order, and this need was reflected in the layout of the Benedictine gardens, which form part of an orderly, well-structured monastery. The Benedictine gardening tradition derives from Italy, where the Benedictine order was founded. Across the Mediterranean region and the Middle East there were strong gardening traditions, well represented by the gardens of Roman villas and in the influential walled gardens of Persia, and it is likely that the Benedictines inherited this tradition. The Benedictine monks differed from the Irish monks in that they seem to have evinced no liking for wilderness, but preferred a regulated landscape, which for them expressed the value of an ordered life and looked forward to heaven.

Benedictine monasteries are designed for order. They are centred on the monastic church, connected with which is the cloister, a courtyard/garden surrounded by porticoes. Comparison with the Roman atrium leaps out, as cloisters descend from this Latin architectural feature. The cloister is a place for meditative prayer and study, either sitting or walking, and it is a private space closed to outsiders. Spreading from the church is a well-ordered set of buildings, dormitories and workshops and gardens. Beyond these lie the monastic farms, if they have them. Order characterizes the structure of the monastery. It is a place for a regular life lived under the monastic rule. Monastic gardening reflects this regularity. Well-ordered beds are planted and tended; flowers, trees and vegetables have their places, being planted for food, healing and worship. Benedictine monasteries reflect the view that faith manifests itself in order and that we encounter God in civilised conditions. The Benedictine view seems contrary to the Irish view, as it grew from a different culture and reflects a different religious experience.

The classic Benedictine monastery is modelled on St Gall [4.] The monastery is centred on the abbey church, a cross-shaped building around which the other edifices cluster. The sacred geometry of church building prescribes that the sanctuary end of the church will be at the East, pointing towards Jerusalem, and at this end there was often a garden known as paradise. This was an ornamental garden intended to be a foretaste of the heavenly paradise to come. St Gall had two paradise gardens, east and west; why this was so is unknown, but as it was originally a Celtic foundation established by Gall, a companion of the ever-wandering Columbanus, the western paradise garden might hark back to the Irish tradition of looking to the sacred west. At the east of the monastery there was the vegetable garden, which was divided into neat beds. There was also a physic garden, in which the infirmarers grew his healing herbs. Nearby was the orchard, in which fruit and nut trees were grown. The orchard doubled up as the burial garden. The monks were usually buried in sheets, so the decomposing bodies nourished the soil in which the trees were growing, and unhampered by coffins, the nutrients from the decomposing bodies reached the tree roots quite quickly. The practice of planting vines in graveyards or burying bodies in vineyards or orchards was long established in the Mediterranean world, and the monasteries were merely continuing this custom. Next to the monastic church was the central garden, the cloister garth, which was a place of prayer and reflection. It is worth noting that the ducks and geese were kept near the vegetable gardens, as their manure would be used as fertiliser. It is important to note that the St Gall plan is merely a list of features to be included rather than a strictly prescribed design. Benedictine monasteries were not designed like Roman forts, which were identical no matter where in the Empire you went. As long as the features were present, their layout could vary quite greatly.

The St Gall plan was not the only monastic layout, but became an exemplar. Certainly prior to this layout, many monasteries had no cloisters and therefore no cloister gardens. Jarrow, for example, the home of St Bede, has been revealed as being a number of buildings and gardens clustered round churches, according to archaeological study. The monastery at Jarrow was originally an Irish foundation, so its design shared the slightly relaxed architectural attitude of the Celtic Church, which evangelised northern Britain prior to the arrival of St Augustine with Roman Christianity in the south of England.

Some monasteries differed from the plan outlined above. Carthusian monasteries were laid out according to this plan, but the gardens were designed to meet the needs of their peculiar way of life. Carthusian priests live in cells and are effectively hermits who meet only for prayer; the brothers, non-ordained monks, manage the monastery and serve the priests. Their monasteries are small, comprising but a few monks. Their cells open at one side onto a corridor, along which the abbot could walk to supervise his monks, and on the other onto the central garden, the cloister garth. The Carthusians maintain gardens just as other monasteries do. The priests do some gardening, but to maintain their solitary lifestyle each has his own private plot on which he cultivates vegetables.

These small gardens are clustered around the cloister garth, which remains an open space in the middle. They serve the vital function of providing fresh air and exercise for these scholarly contemplative monks who spend most of the day in private study and prayer. The Carthusians may seem to be a strange group of people, but they have one boast: they are the only order in the Catholic Church which has never been reformed, because they are the only order that never needed reformation. Their history has been scandal-free. Of course, if you are enclosed in a cell for most of the day, there is little opportunity to do anything scandalous. The small gardens serve as not only a means of growing the monks' rations, but also as exercise. Scholars they may be, but their bodies need exercise just as everyone else's bodies do.

The now-extinct Cluniacs were a branch of the Benedictines who spent more time at prayer than the Benedictines did, particularly in church services. Their monasteries and gardens were laid out along Benedictine lines, but they hired servants to do much of the manual work.

The Cistercians [colloquially known as Trappists] were not primarily gardeners. As their rule enjoins strict silence, they sought out lonely places to establish their monasteries. These places they turned into farms, in Britain often for sheep, hence they flourished from the wool trade. They were farmers more than gardeners. This is not to say that they did not garden, far from it, but the main thrust of Cistercian activity was farming. There was good reasoning for this preference. The lands that they took at first were often marginal and far more suitable for sheep farming than for the more intense tillage involved in gardening, so an emphasis on farming was economically necessary.

They were deeply involved in the English wool trade and thus were an integral part of the economy of mediaeval England. We can find their traces today in the many places with the name Grange included in their name. A Grange was an outlying farm belonging to a Cistercian abbey. These could be several miles from the parent foundation. Sometimes their buildings were used for storage, but generally in England sheep were kept on their lands. One peculiar Cistercian rule is that the order refused to have corn mills. This rule caused some problems when the Cistercians merged with the Savignacs in the late twelfth century, as the latter had mills. Eventually agreement was reached in which the ex-Savignac monasteries retained their mills, but later foundations maintained the Cistercian rule on the matter. Effectively this rule deterred Cistercian foundations from growing corn, as milling was expensive if you had to buy it in from an outside source.

There are Benedictine and Carthusian nuns, who live in convents separate from the monks, but the Cistercian order originally refused to have a female branch, though there is one now. Everything said of the monks' gardens applies to nuns' gardens as well. Sadly there survives almost nothing written about the nuns' gardens, but considering that women were serious gardeners right through the mediaeval period, it is likely that convent gardens were richly productive places. It is also likely that convents were based in or near urban areas, because the countryside in the mediaeval period was not the safest of places, especially for a group of women. It is harder to find remains in town than it is in the country, as they are often built over.

Convents were generally poorer than monasteries, so it is likely that the sisters did much of the garden work themselves, but it is possible that they hired servants for the physically heavy tasks, such as the annual digging of the ground in Spring, which was a task traditionally done by men. A sympathetic local lord may have lent men to help out at certain times of the year. Certainly the long association between women and the healing arts may have meant that convents had richly productive herb gardens. These would have served the sick of the local community and provided a source of income for the nuns. There are a few records. William Rufus, whose distinction as a king was that he was probably even worse than Henry the Eighth, visited a convent at Romsey ostensibly to smell the roses in the garden, but probably to "visit" twelve-year-old Matilda, the future wife of Henry, his brother. The abbess, who happened to be her aunt Christine, managed to dress her as a nun when she heard the knights riding into the convent; and so the girl was not harmed. However, this does show that there was a well-kept garden there at an early date. Furthermore, we also find that the hospital in Norwich the nuns had good gardens. They had a "great garden" and a kitchen garden, the term great probably indicating that it was large. The nuns also had both ornamental garden and a paradise garden [see below for an explanation of the paradise] along with a fishpond. They also kept pigs and possessed a meadow. Whether they kept cattle in the meadow or simply rented it out we do not know. Renting would have been a good source of cash for them, and as the poor would not have paid for medical treatment, a source of cash would have been needed.

There were and are other monastic orders, some of which are extinct and others were never in the British Isles. In an English context it is important to remember the Gilbertines, the only English monastic order ever established. They had twenty-four houses in Lincolnshire and none anywhere else. Records of their farming can still be found, but no gardening records exist. There was probably nothing distinct about their gardening model.

The layout of monastic gardens

Gardens suit the monastic lifestyle, which is somewhat secluded from the world. While monks are not totally cut off from the world outside the monastery, they value their privacy. Gardens have always tended to be enclosed spaces, as the early walled gardens of Persia show. The word garth, an early English word for garden, is linked to the words girth, gird and gard, the latter being a fortified place in Scandinavian languages, and indicating a place <u>girded</u> round with a fence. Hortus, the Latin word for garden, is etymologically related to garth, as H and G tend to interchange in some instances. Also interchangeable are Y and G, a fact that indicates that the word garden is also related to the word yard. Early gardens were fenced off against intruders, notably wild animals, raiders and thieves. Hence the monastic garden was a hortus conclusus, a closed garden. Monastic gardens in Anglo-Saxon England would have been fenced with wattle and daub or thorn hedges Later on some gardens were contained behind monastery walls.

The discussion that follows will focus on gardens as they were in the heyday of monasticism in the Middle Ages, at which period the essential design of monasteries became formalised. Many features still remain, with modifications to suit changing circumstances. Manual labour still has a place in the monastery; several still have farms; and most if not all have some kind of garden. Monasteries being smaller now than they were, fewer of the activities that are described below are feasible because of manpower shortages, and many monasteries now focus their economic activity on small craft industries. Crops are generally now grown for purely internal consumption, as it is hard for small institutions to make a profit in the modern market for foodstuffs. However, at Buckfast Abbey in South West England they still produce and sell a tonic wine flavoured with their own herbs.

Monastic horticulture has kept up with the times and has always been open to new varieties and techniques. While there were, for example, no potatoes in Mediaeval Europe, monasteries took them up as fast as anyone else did. There is no research on the impact of the organic movement on monastic horticulture, but it is likely that the unmaterialistic monks would be keen not to poison the earth with excessive pesticides, though there is nothing to imply that Catholic or Christian doctrine should support organic horticulture, other than the principle that humans are bound to do what is best for the world and its people.

Paradise

Monastic churches generally had a Paradise, a beautiful garden intended to be a memory of the Garden of Eden, before sin entered the world, when the world was as it ought to be. This was at one end of the church. There were ornamental flowers and shrubs, maybe even trees. The paradise might overlap with other kinds of monastic garden, thus it might have fruit trees and healing herbs, and it did sometimes serve as a sacristan's garden [see below.] It might even be the burial garden, symbolizing that the dead monks had entered paradise. The paradise was intended to be a spiritual experience, a place conducive to meditation and spiritual thoughts.

The Cloister Garth

This is at the heart of the monastery, and its structure has not changed since cloisters were established. The layout of cloisters is derived from a Roman villa. A series of covered walkways surrounds and looks over a square garden. The walkways are designed as places where monks may sit or walk, reflecting and praying as they do so, and it is common to see monks walking and reading a book there. Yet the garden at the middle is a sacred space into which few venture except to tend plants. While there is no rule against entering this cloister garth, monks generally do not do so. It is a sacred place, a symbol of the great mystery of God, the invisible presence at the heart of the monastery. It is symbolic of the mystery that lies at the heart of prayer, the formlessness of God, encountered in prayer but transcending adequate description. It therefore prompts reflection on the divine mystery.

The garth was and still is often a lawn, known in the mediaeval period as a laund, though there may be paths across it in the form of a cross, dividing the garden into quarters, symbolizing the ordered character of creation under God's governance, and a sign that order in heaven should be reflected in the orderly lives of people on Earth. The Mediaevals did not have the desire for lawns trimmed short, as is the modern fashion, and so during that period the grass could be reasonably long. The fashion for trimmed lawns arose because the squires who succeeded the monks as landowners could afford to have servants trimming the grass with scissors. The monks probably scythed it occasionally. During the Mediaeval period lawns were sometimes planted with bulbs, so that flowers would go through them. There is sometimes a pool or fountain at its heart. Water has deep religious symbolism. It symbolizes baptism, spiritual cleanliness and the living water of which Christ spoke [5.] Pools may symbolize the tranquillity of mystical prayer[b] As a pool has depths concealed below its surface, so God has infinite depths, the shallows of which the prayerful might plumb. Some cloister garths have ornamental box hedging, maybe in a maze to suggest the mystery of God. A statue of Christ might be at the centre of the cloister garth, to show that while God is invisible Christ makes him known. [c]

Sometimes the cloister garth serves other monastic purposes. Monasteries with little land used it as a herbarium. Carthusian monasteries use it as a burial plot, so the dead brothers remain at the heart of the monastery.

A cloister garth: The wall is cut through to obtain a view of the garden. The herbs indicate that it is a small priory.

---

[b] Mystical prayer is a state of deep union with the ultimate/cosmic whole in which individuality is submerged for a period of time. It is ineffable, a state beyond description in language.
[c] Bonaventure, a mediaeval Franciscan thinker, stated that Christ was the centre and the axis of creation.

The cloister garth serves as a light well for the cloisters, which have no windows onto the outside world so as to prevent distractions from entering the monastery. Within many cloisters are carrels, small recesses where there are seats for monks to read. Such seats need to back onto a window to provide light for reading, which the empty space of the cloister garth provides. The background silence of the cloister garth is an important condition for quiet reading. Benedictines, who love scholarship, would have found this kind of garden a good background for study.

The Sacristan's Garden

Many monasteries had a sacristan's garden. A sacristan is an official whose role is to prepare the church services. As Catholic services are adorned with flowers, his job involved planting and cutting flowers. He would have to select the flowers appropriate to the liturgy [formal worship] of the day. This involved picking blooms of the right colour, where possible. While there are no rules as to what flowers [or colours of flowers] are used, Catholic mass vestments are colour-coded according to the festival/saint celebrated on the day: red for martyrs, white for Confessors [other saints], green for ordinary days, purple for Lent and Advent, blue for feasts of Mary and gold for Christmas and Easter [though in many churches white suffices.] Black was until the 1960s used at funerals, but obviously no flowers are of this colour. Matching the flower with the liturgical colour was desirable, though not always possible, and a skilled sacristan gardener might well have a range of flowers of appropriate colours. It is likely that on some special religious festivals the priests celebrating mass wore wreaths of flowers, just as ancient Romans had worn laurel wreaths.

Scent may also have been a consideration in the selection of plants for adorning services. The Roman Catholic, Orthodox and some Anglican churches use incense in some of their ceremonies; and this indicates that they believe that there is a place for scents in worship. They believe that all senses can be involved in the worshipping experience and so they are happy to use them. While there are no rules as to the use of scented flowers in ceremonies, there have never been any objections to the practice. A good sacristan might well have selected flowers that were producing beautiful scents to enrich the aesthetic quality of the services. Sadly, there is nothing written on this subject.

In recent years a charitable trust has recreated a Sacristan's garden with the plants that would have been available in the fifteenth century. The garden is situated inside the remains of the old monastic church. The Saint Lawrence Centre for Training and the Arts at South Walsham in Norfolk, midway between Great Yarmouth and Norwich, is part of the quiet gardens project, which establishes gardens as places of reflection and mental recuperation. Situated on the B1140 between Paxworth and Acle, it is well worth a visit. I am basing my account of the sacristan's garden on information kindly supplied by the Trust, but with additional comments. While it is not clear that the mediaeval Sacristan there grew all these flowers, they would have been available to him

Planting list
These plants have been planted in the Walsham Sacristan's garden.

Spring flowering
Adonis annua: yellow flowers
Allium ursinum: [wild garlic] White flowers in spring

Angelica archangelica: white flowers in spring.

Chelidonium majus: [Great Celandine, swallow wort, tetterwort] Yellow flowers

Convallaria majalis [Lily of the Valley] Lilies have always been a plant with biblical associations, having been mentioned by Jesus in the Sermon on the Mount. They are also associated with Mary, for their whiteness indicates purity. The white flowers bloom in spring.

Cheiranthus cheiri: orange foliage

Dryopteris felix-mas [male fern] Copper red fronds in spring give way to green growth in summer.

Erysimum: This member of the cabbage family produces orange flowers.

Euphorbia polychrome: This plant produces bright yellow flowers.

Euphorbia amygdaloides robbiae: [wood spurge] Yellow flowers.

Filipendula ulmaria [meadowsweet.] Bright golden-yellow flowers in spring give way to green in summer. This was also grown in the brewer's garden.

Paeonia officionalis: [Peony] Red flowers.

Polygonum bistorta [Bistort.] White/pinkish flowers. This was often used as a bitter herb for Lenten eating.

Primula veris [cowslip] Pendulous beautifully scented yellow blooms are produced.

Primula vulgaris [primrose] Beautiful yellow and white flowers
Symphytum officinale [comfrey] Comfrey bears pale blue flowers tinged with pink.

Spring to summer

Anemone pulsatilla: White flowers tinged with blue or pink in late spring to early summer.

Genista tinctoria: [dyer's greenweed.] Golden-yellow flowers bloom from late spring into summer.
Hesperis matronalis [Dame's violet, sweet rocket] White flowers bloom from late spring to early summer.
Iris germanica var. florentina: Blue flowers grow from late spring to early summer.
Myosotis sylvatica: Tiny blue flowers are produced from late spring to early summer
Polymonium Caeruleum [Jacob's ladder] this name has biblical associations, as the name refers to the story of Jacob in Genesis, who saw a ladder reaching to heaven. Purple flowers similar to blue bell emerge in May to June.
Calendula officionalis: [marigold.] This was common also in Marian gardens [see below]. Yellow and orange flowers running from spring to early autumn
Pulmonaria officionalis [lungwort] Long, dark-blue flowers grow from Feb/March to June
Rosmarinus officionalis [Rosemary.] This evergreen plant flowers from spring into summer and sometimes into early autumn.
Vinca minor [periwinkle.] The small, pale-yellow flowers begin in mid spring, but can continue until early autumn.
Viola tricolor [wild pansy, heartsease.] The flowers, which are violet to the point of being black, begin in spring and run through to autumn

Summer flowering
Achillea millefolium: Rich red flowers are produced.
Aconitum napellus [Monkshood, wolf bane] a plant poisonous but beautiful, with light indigo blue flowers
Alchemilla vulgaris: Greenish yellow flowers are produced.

Allium schoenoprasum: [chives]. The flowers of chives are a pleasant purple or pink. Chives maybe planted in the vegetable garden or herbarium as well

Anethum graveolens [dill.] This culinary herb produces yellowish green flowers in summer.

Aquilegia vulgaris: pink, crimson, purple or white flowers in early summer

Arnica Montana: [Leopard's bane.] This yellow perennial is difficult to grow, but it has been widely used for healing bruises and sprains.

Artemisia absinthum: grown for its silvery grey foliage, the flower heads are insignificant.

Artemesia abrotanum: Silvery grey foliage, but bears small yellow flowers in late summer

Bellis perennis [Daisy] white and yellow flower heads in early summer

Calamintha grandiflora: Calamintha produces purple flowers throughout summer and into autumn.

Chamaemelum nobile [Roman Camomile] White flowers in summer

Cichorium intybus: [chicory.] This plant has light blue flowers in summer.

Coriandrum sativum: coriander. This could well have grown also in herbaria, as it is a spice. The flowers are white.

Cynoglossum officionale [houndstongue] Light blue flowers from late spring to early autumn.

Dianthus caryophillus [both clove pink and white forms]

Digitalis purpurea [foxglove.] This plant is beautiful, but poisonous. The flowers are pink, red, purple or white.

Carum carvi: This white flowered plant known as caraway is used as a spice, but was never common in Britain

Aster x Frikartii: tubular reddish pink flowers

Echium vulgare: This dwarf plant produces lowers of pink, white, blue and purple.

Eryngium maritinum: [Sea holly.] Probably more common in coastal areas, this plant was grown mainly for its foliage.

Feoniculum vulgare: [fennel.] Fennel had a place in different kinds of garden. Infirmarers also grew this plant. It has edible roots and leaves. Its flowers are yellow and some varieties have bronze foliage.

Frageria vesca [wild strawberry] White flowers bloom in summer.

Galega officinalis [goat's rue.] The flowers of this herb are lilac-mauve and white.

Gallium odoratum   [woodruff.] Woodruff produces carpets of star shaped small white flowers.

Hyssopus officionalis: Hyssop had a role in Catholic services, as it was used to sprinkle holy water at the Easter vigil, which takes place on Holy Saturday evening before midnight mass, the first mass of Easter. Densely packed dark blue flowers grow from midsummer to early autumn

Lavandula angustifolia "Hidcote" Densely packed blue flowers grow from mid to late summer.

Lavandula spica: This species produces tall purple-blue flowers.

Linum perenne: Funnel-shaped clear blue flowers attract bees and so were important in attracting pollinators to the garden.

Lonicera periclymenum: [Honeysuckle, woodbine.] Long-tubed dark purple flowers with a pink inside grow in mid to late summer. As nectar rich plants they attract bees.

Malva moschata This short -lived perennial produces saucer shaped rose pink flowers in early summer

Melissa officinalis: [lemon balm] Bright golden yellow leaves grow on this popular herb.

Mentha pulegium [creeping penny royal.] Purple flowers grow in summer

Mentha spicata [spearmint.] Pink or white flowers grow in late summer to early autumn.

Mentha suaveolens [apple mint.] This herb was not grown for its flowers, which it rarely produces. Mints in general were grown for scent. Perhaps this is an indication that scent was valued in mediaeval monastic church services

Mentha x piperata: Pink flowers are less important than the scent of this species.

Myrrhis odorata [sweet cicely.] This herb produces white flowers in early summer, lush green foliage and a strong scent.

Nepeta cataria [catmint.] This plant was grown for its silver-grey foliage and its spiked flowers of violet spotted white.

Nigella sativa [Black cumin] Pale blue flowers are less significant than the scent of this powerful herb.

Origanum majorana: [Sweet marjoram.] This was grown mainly for its grey-green foliage.

Papaver rhoeas [corn poppy.] This common and easily grown plant has reddish leaves with a white interior.

Papaver somniferum [opium poppy] The opium poppy produces flowers ranging through red, pink, purple and white.

Petroselinum crispum [parsley.] Primarily a culinary herb, the foliage may have been used in churches.

Plantago major [plantain.] The inflorescence is greenish yellow.

Rosa X Alba "White Rose of York" Roses of various kinds would have been as common as they are today.

Ruta graveolens [rue.] This is not an attractive plant, so it is possible that its strong and unpleasant smell was used to deter vermin from churches rather than ornament services.

Salvia officinalis [sage] Small blue flowers are produced.
Salvia officinalis "purpurescens" Flowers are purple rather than blue.
Santolina chamaecyparissus [cotton lavender.] Mid to late summer sees bright yellow flowers emerge.
Saponaria officinalis [soapwort] Red flowers are produced in summer.
Satureja Montana [savory.] Lavender flowers are produced in summer.
Sedum acre [stonecrop.] Produces tiny yellow flowers
Sempervivum tectorum: This alpine plant produces star shaped yellow flowers
Thymus serpyllum: Probably grown mainly for scent, thyme produce small purple flowers
Thymus vulgaris [Thyme] As above, this plant was probably grown primarily for scent.
Thymus x citriodorus: This thyme has a more citrus-like scent.
Valerian officinalis: known as a healing herb, it has purple flowers in June to July.
Verbascum thapsus [Great Mullein; Aaron's Rod] The name has biblical associations, Aaron being the brother of Moses. This tall plant produces densely packed yellow flowers.

Summer to autumn
Borago officinalis [Borage.] Blue flowers in summer to early autumn
Centaurea cyanus [cornflower.] The blue, pink red and purple flowers bloom in late summer to early autumn.
Tanacetum parthenium [feverfew.] This short-lived perennial has daisy white flowers and green-gold leaves. The foliage may have been more important than the flowers.

Tanacetum vulgare [tansey] Yellow flower heads emerge from July to October.

Teucrium chamaedris [wall germander] Pale pink to deep purple flowers grow from June to September.

Autumn

Aster amellus: Deep blue flower heads with yellow centres

Humulus lupulus "Aureus" [Golden hop] Golden flowers are produced in autumn.

Winter to spring

Helleborus niger: [Christmas rose.] This white hellebore would have been important for its blossoms at a time when flowers were few.

Viola odorata [sweet violet] White or violet flowers are produced. This plant would have been useful as an alternative to helleborus.

Other

Taxus x media "Hicksii" [yew.] Yew was in pre-Christian times a plant that symbolised life after death on account of its longevity, which is why it is found in churchyards, an example of how the Catholic faith took up older traditions and transformed them. In sacristans' gardens it was probably a hedging plant

Vitis vinifera "Purpurescens" [grape vine.] there is only one use for the grape vine, which is wine It may have been grown in monasteries without vineyards.

Malus [apple] Pinkish flowers grow in spring.

Some of these plants we will meet in other sections; and it is likely that as some of them have medicinal use as they were found in the physic garden. In fact, the number of herbs grown in sacristans' gardens indicates that there might have been an overlap between the sacristan's garden and the physic garden in some monasteries, probably the smaller ones. However, they are all planted in the sacristan's garden at Walsham, so they are included here. It is very likely that the range of plants grown in a monastery garden was dependent upon local availability and the Sacristan's personal choice, subject to his duty of obedience to the abbot. Sometimes the Paradise was used as the sacristan's garden; and at other times the Sacristan had the Marian garden.

That one or two are poisonous, for example Aconite [monkshood], did not deter the monks from using them. The monks believed that every being in some sense reflected God's glory and so had a place in the world. Thomas Aquinas, the great theologian whose teachings have long shaped Catholic Theology, argued that every being in some sense resembled the creator and therefore had a purpose, a work that it had to fulfil. It might be beautiful to look at and so could rightly adorn church services. The rule was to use each being properly for the well being of humans and the glory of God.

The Marian garden

Mary the mother of Jesus has enjoyed enormous status in the Roman Catholic and Orthodox churches, probably because people need to honour a sacred feminine, and so as God is described as male, there is an emotional need for a feminine object of devotion. This lack of a divine feminine is an unnecessary deficiency in Christian thinking. The Old Testament says that God made male and female in his own image and likeness, so God must have equally feminine and masculine qualities. However, the religious language used to describe

God tends to be masculine, so the divine feminine is often overlooked. Mary fills the devotional gap left by the missing feminine side of God. Certainly she has been and still is the object of many devotions. The English were deeply devoted to Mary during the mediaeval period and devotion continued until the Reformation suppressed it. Monastic devotions in honour of her were therefore common. As a feminine figure she is seen to have a natural affinity with flowers.

Some monasteries had a Marian garden, in honour of Mary the mother of Christ and stocked with plants associated with her. This was metaphorically the Virgin's Bower. It was not always distinct from the Sacristan's garden. For example at Melrose, an abbey in Scotland which was dedicated to Mary, the Marian garden was the sacristan's garden [6.] At Norwich Cathedral Priory the Sacristan had the Marian garden.[d]

At Melrose the Sacristan grew rosemary, a plant whose name indicates that is sacred to Mary, and even the rarer blue rosemary, whose blue colour makes it especially apt for Mary, the statues of whom often depict her wearing blue. Roses and lilies are also mentioned, the lily being in honour of Mary's purity.

The following plants are associated with Mary and may have grown in Marian gardens:

---

[d] Priories differ from abbeys. Both are monasteries, but abbeys are ruled by an abbot, the highest monastic office, whereas priories are ruled by a prior, a person of lower rank. Priories were smaller than abbeys and are best seen as outlying institutions dependent upon an abbey, whose abbot would exercise supervisory authority over them. They had a smaller range of resources than abbeys had.

Planting time: April

scientific name	modern name	religious name
Campanula medium	Canterbury bells	Our Lady's nightcap
Bellis perennis	English daisy	Mary-loves
Digitalis purpurea	Foxglove	Our Lady's gloves
Althea rosea	Hollyhock	St Joseph's staff
Viola tricolor	Pansy	Our Lady's delight
Dianthus barbatus	Sweet William	Our Lady's cushion
Gypsophila paniculata	Baby's breath	Our Lady's veil
Dicentra spectabilis	Bleeding heart	Mary's heart
Dianthus plumaris	Clove pink	Virgin pink
Aquilegia vulgaris	Columbine	Our Lady's shoes
Primula veris	Cowslip primrose	Our Lady's keys
Myosotes scorpoides	Forget-me-not	Eyes of Mary
Iris	Iris	Mary's sword of sorrow
Primula elatior	Primrose	Mary's candlestick
Lynchis coronaria	Rose campion	Mary's rose
Armeria maritima	Sea pink	Our Lady's pincushion
Polygonatum multifarium	Solomon's seal	Our Lady's lockets
Tradescantia Virginia	Spiderwort	Our Lady's tears
Frageria vesca	Strawberry	Fruitful virgin
Veronica maritima	Veronica	Our Lady's faith
Viola odorata	Violet	Our Lady's modesty

May:

scientific name	modern name	religious name
Aurinia saxatile	Alyssum	Mary's flower
Amaranthus tricolor	Amaranthus	Joseph's coat
Impatiens balsamium	Balsam	Our Lady's slipper
Silene armeria	Catch-fly	Mary's rose
Chrysanthemum segetum	Chrysanthemum	Mary's gold
Centaurea cyanis	Cornflower	Mary's crown
Papaver rhoeas	Corn poppy	Mary's buttons

Gaillardia pulchella	Gallardia	The virgin's face
Delphinium ajacis	Larkspur	Mary's tears
Tagetes	Marigold	Mary's gold
Ipomea purpurea	Morning glory	Our Lady's mantle
Tropaeolum majus	Nasturtium	St Joseph's flower
Nigella damascena	Love-in-a-mist	Our Lady in the shade
Impatiens wallerana	Patient Lucy	Mother Love
Petunia	Petunia	Our Lady's praises
Calendula officionalis	Pot marigold	Mary's gold
Briza maxima	Quaking grass	Our Lady's braids
Scabiosa atropurpurea	Scabious	Our Lady's pincushion
Antirrhinum majus	Snapdragon	Infant Jesus' shoes
Mathiola incana	Stock	Our Lady's violet
Helthanus annus	Sunflower	Mary's gold
Lathyrus odoratus	Sweet pea	Our Lady's flower
Zinnia elegans	Zinnia	The Virgin

It is important to note that these plants have no biblical or theological connection with Mary. Their Marian connection arises solely from folk tradition. Plants once linked with the Great Goddess, the oldest deity worshipped by the human race and still worshipped across Europe in the mediaeval period [and today by some modern pagans] were simply transferred to Mary, often with the compliance of the church, which realized that it was more productive to use folk traditions than to fight them. This was the case when Catholicism simply took over the old pagan ritual year, placing important Christian feasts on the dates of older pagan ones. It is worth noting that on Mayday, feast given over to Mary, churches used to be bedecked with flowers.

The productive gardens

The gardens that are discussed in this section produced food, herbs and other useful plants. For convenience they are discussed in terms of medicine and food, but the division between vegetable garden and physic garden was not absolute. Sometimes the herbs, medicinal, culinary and otherwise, were grown in a herbarium while culinary vegetables were grown in the vegetable garden. But they cannot be treated in isolation from the monastery farm[s] orchard [pomerium] and fishing activities, which had a bearing upon what vegetables were grown in the garden. Central to the whole set of activities was the monastic diet. The Benedictines were originally vegetarian, but they modified this prohibition in the light of the practicalities of life, especially in northern climes, where meat eating might be a necessity in winter and in some areas with soils less productive than those of benign Italy. Monks, however, ate predominantly simple dishes, such as potage and mixt, a light meal serving as breakfast or lunch.

Porray, which is a hash of vegetables and meat boiled together, was often eaten. There were several kinds of porray. One recipe for green porray advises that peas be boiled until tender and then kept warm. They are then mixed with chopped onions and sprigs of parsley in equal amounts. Some sage leaves are added. They are then boiled together with vine vinegar and just before serving diced bread is added. The proportions in the recipe are: 5 onion and 5 parsley springs; 2 sage leaves; two teaspoons of vinegar; and four slices of diced bread. However, the serving for a monastery would require larger amounts and the precise amounts cannot be ascertained. There were other kinds of porray. White porray used leeks and ham. Sometimes milk was an ingredient, especially on fish days.

On the farms monks kept cattle for milk and cheese, Cistercian farms bred sheep in abundance, primarily for wool, but possibly for milk. Grain would have been grown on the farms. Chickens were also kept at many monasteries, and their manure would have been used in the gardens. Turnips seem not to have been grown in monastery gardens, but they almost certainly grew on the farms on field scale.

Bees formed an important part of the monastic economy, and still do at Buckfast Abbey, where the late Brother Adam, an internationally renowned beekeeper, made them into an abbey specialism. Bees were needed for candles, for Catholic liturgical candles must be made from beeswax, and also for their honey, which in the days before the availability of sugar was the main sweetener. Hives would have certainly made the tour of monastery gardens and farms according to the availability of nectar, and there would have been consultation between monastic gardeners and beekeepers as to the right time and place for the beehives to be sited. Monastic hives would have been important pollinators for many plants, ensuring that plants requiring insect pollination flourished. Considering that the Sacristan's and Marian gardens were full of flowers, many of which would be nectar-bearing species that rely on insect pollination, the hives would have spent quite some time in these gardens. Sacristan, kitchen gardener and beekeeper needed to work closely together.

Yet it was not only for beeswax that the monks kept bees. Honey was an important sweetener in the days before cane sugar was discovered. It was also an ingredient of several brews. Some of these may well have been used by the infirmarer in his work for the sick. Metheglyn is basically mead, fermented honey, with healing herbs included. [The word is Welsh for medicine.]

Mediaeval societies developed a tradition of using waste far more so than modern throwaway cultures. Even until the nineteenth century great country houses buried their domestic "soil" in the gardens. Collecting the night soil was a morning task for the junior gardeners, and the monastery toilets, the garderobes, would have their contents buried in the garden as fertiliser. It is most likely that monasteries used the traditional method of composting, which was to bury the waste in a trench, which was then filled in. Before the development of composting proper, plant remains were left in the road to be walked or ridden on to break them so as to render their decay quicker. Food waste was probably fed to pigs, which were kept on the farms.

The plan of the abbey of St Gall, which dates from the years 815-820, depicts a small area in which herbs and vegetables were not separated into specialist gardens, and there seems to have been no distinction between culinary herbs and medicinal herbs. The garden was located between the orchard/cemetery and the chickens and geese, probably for easier transport of manure.

The garden was divided into 18 beds. Some rotation would have been necessary, so this is what they would have been like in the year that the chart was drawn:

Onions	**Garlic**
Leeks	**Shallots**
Celery	**Parsley**
Coriander	**Chervil**
Dill	**Lettuce**
Poppy	**Savory**
Radish	**Parsnip**
Carrot	**Cabbage**
Beet	**Corncockle**

Many of these plants are included in the Capitulare of Charlemagne, a list of plants that he wanted included in his palace garden. The exception is carrot, which is not native to Europe and which probably came from the East in the first millennium C.E. Corncockle is a surprising inclusion. It is not eaten and has no medicinal uses. However, it is bitter, so it might have been used as flavouring for beer.

The beds seem to be narrow enough to allow a gardener on the path to reach to the centre, although what they lost in width they seem to have made up in length. . The sides were probably boarded and the soil level therefore elevated above the level of the path. Tended over many years this makes for beds that have a friable, rich tilth in which crops grow abundantly. It is interesting to see that the raised bed system was in use in monastic gardens at this early date. It is evidence that monastic horticulture was practised by gardeners who thought about the best way to grow their plants.

From England we find the work of Aelfric of Eynsham, a teacher who wrote a vocabulary list that was preserved by his student Aelfric Batta in 995. This is useful as it gives a list of garden plants grown in the period. They include Ficus [fig] known as Fic beam, peach, known as Persoc Treow, and Vine, known as Win Treow.

At very large monasteries, such as Beaulieu, specialist gardens developed quite quickly to meet the needs of specific activities. There was a large kitchen garden and an infirmary garden, but there were a dozen other gardens linked to various monastic activities, including some mentioned above. One of which was a brewer's garden, which produced the bitter herbs used to flavour ale.

The Vegetable Garden

The vegetable garden had to feed a place with sometimes over a hundred men living in it, so it must have been a major enterprise that worked in conjunction with the monastery farms. We must not think that vegetable gardens were always behind the monastery walls. At Shrewsbury the vegetable garden was outside the abbey walls, although adjoining the abbey. It was part of a large unit with the orchard and the abbey farm where corn was grown and sheep were kept. It is noteworthy that the distinction between agriculture and horticulture, which has grown with the tendency to increasing specialisation, was not as clear in the mediaeval period as it is now. All family farms had a vegetable garden adjoining the house and the farming and horticultural activities were regarded as aspects of the whole family activity.

The following vegetables were known in Mediaeval Britain and generally across Europe and so may have grown in the monastery vegetable gardens:

Alexander has been known in Britain since the Romans introduced it. It is an herb of coastal regions and so may have been grown in monasteries near to the sea. Its prime use is in salads and as a garnish.
Beans: Both broad and kidney beans were known and made an ideal ingredient for potage. They were also dried for winter use.
Beet: The Saint Gall documents show that beet was sometimes grown in monastery gardens. Beetroot can be peeled and boiled to make an excellent bulk vegetable. It is important to bear in mind that beetroot was not simply the standard red kind that we have now, as there are

yellow and white varieties that were once common. Sugar beet was not known in Britain in the mediaeval period.

Bistort: It was an ancient custom long pre-dating Christianity to eat bitter herbs in the early spring. The Jews eat bitter herbs at Passover, and the custom seems to have been common elsewhere. There was a folk belief that these herbs are purgatives that purify the bodies and minds of those who eat them.

Cabbage/kale/colewort were early versions of the modern varieties and were not yet bred to the same size as modern cabbages. As a plant that can grow throughout the year they formed an important ingredient of the monastic diet. The vitamin C contained therein would have provided a defence against scurvy.

Carrot: A staple in any diet, carrots will grow into winter and early spring and so would have been a good vegetable for the hungry period at the end of winter. However, it was not known in Britain until the fifteenth century, when it was introduced by Flemish refugees. We must not think that at that time carrots were exclusively orange, for there were purple, red, white, yellow, green and black varieties. In fact the orange carrot was bred after the mediaeval period. Originally carrots were quite thin, and it is only as the years have progressed that breeders have developed thicker varieties.

Celery: This vegetable is mentioned in the description of the monastery of St Gall in 815. It was important in salads.

Chervil would have been used as flavouring for potage. It was grown at St Gall.

Chives were also known in the mediaeval period.

Coriander: This was an herb popular with monks. Its leaves were added to salad and its seeds to bread. However, it might not have grown across Britain, being an herb needing a warmer climate.

Garlic: This vegetable was used to flavour cooked dishes, but its herbal uses will be detailed below.

Leek: In Britain, especially the North of England, Scotland and Wales, leeks are a vital vegetable. Their ability to grow in winter and into February and makes them an essential winter staple.

Lettuce: This was a great staple salad vegetable. However, modern lettuce has been bred for blandness compared with its wild ancestor, which acted as a soporific.

Lovage was an herb with an important role in flavouring potage.

Mustard was a very popular garden vegetable in monasteries. For some reason mediaeval monks believed that it was important to much of it, and there was often a monastic official known as a mustardarius whose task was to ensure that supplies of mustard were always available.

Onion: Widely known across Europe, onions were a staple part of the mediaeval diet.

Orach, Good King Henry and Fat Hen were widely grown and eaten in Britain from prehistoric times until the nineteenth century, when spinach, which resembles them in taste and which like them belongs to the Chenopodacaea family, took over, so while there is no record of their having been grown in monastery gardens it is likely that they were. Good King Henry was known as Good Henry up to the time of Henry the Eighth, a tyrant whom it was advisable to appease by a suitably grovelling ascription of the word good to his name. Actually the name has nothing to do with him, as it is an old Germanic name [Gutenheinrich] long predating Henry the Eighth. Their leaves are eaten as green vegetables in salad or cooked. They can be diced and added to stews.

Parsnip: At time when potatoes were not known parsnips often served as the bulk vegetable at a meal. The wild variety is native to Britain.

Radish was a spring vegetable quick to grow, and so can be planted to fill a gap in Early spring. It was popular in monastic diets.

Ramson: Known as the poor man's garlic these roots grow widely in Britain and can be grown in gardens. They are used as onions and leeks are and can be used for flavouring potage. However, there is no evidence of their having been grown in monastic gardens.

Rocket was well known in during the mediaeval period and is native to Britain.

Savory was an herb used for flavouring dishes. It was cooked with broad beans. Fish dishes were stuffed with it. This made it an important herb during Lent, when monks could eat no meat.

Scurvy grass: This was in demand for its ability to cure scurvy. It is rich in vitamin C. How many monasteries grew it we do not know.

Sea holly: The roots were eaten in spring, and the leaves in summer. However, as the roots were reputed to be an aphrodisiac it seems likely that the monks stuck to the leaves, we hope.

Silverweed: Only in the Celtic regions of the British Isles was this very nutritious vegetable grown. At Landdwyn Island off Newborough Warren in Anglesey the site of the ruined priory is rich in silverweed, as I can testify from my own observation when I visited the site in summer 2006. Considering that silverweed was popular with the Celtic peoples and that there must have been a monastery garden at the site, it is likely that the monks grew it there and that what I saw was the survival of the monastic vegetable patch, though the precise location of the vegetable garden is not identifiable. The silverweed has spread widely across the site. This vegetable was and is uncommon in England, but silverweed, described in Gaelic as the seventh bread, was known in Somerset and Devon, Western areas where the population was substantially descended from the ancient Britons. Silverweed was eventually replaced by the potato, but it serves the same function in meals, acting as a bulk vegetable.

Shallots: These grow where onions grow. The St Gall description prescribes that a bed be devoted to them.

Strawberry: This native berry was widely known in the mediaeval period, though the larger, sweeter varieties had not yet been bred.

Sweet Cicely: The Romans introduced this herb, which was used for flavourings and salad.

Thyme: This herb was used for flavouring lamb. While monks ate little meat, they ate it occasionally at great feasts, and significant guests may have had it. Abbots often served as diplomats for the king and thus might have had to receive honoured guests who would, as aristocrats, be used to meat, which would have to be seasoned.

Other herbs: There were other herbs that might have grown in monastery herbaria:

Madder: This was a plant that yielded a red dye.

Southernwood: This herb provides an insect and flea repellent.

Rue: The need for hygiene rendered this insecticidal herb very useful.

Rosemary: Rosemary was strewn on church floors to provide a pleasant scent, and it could be burned as incense, which is often used in Catholic services and whose supply from the Middle East, dominated by Muslims, could not always be guaranteed.

The Cellarer's/brewer's Garden

This only sometimes existed, one of the small number of specialist gardens that monasteries sometimes developed in the larger abbeys. The Mediaeval English drank much ale. Ale, however, was brewed then from a range of cereals and was not confined to barley: barley, wheat, oats and rye have also been made into ale. But besides being brewed from a range of cereals, ale could be flavoured with a variety of ingredients, many of which would have been grown by the cellarer. Hops were imported from Flanders in the middle ages, but prior to that a variety of bitter herbs was used. Ivy has been used as an ale-flavouring, as has damson. Alecost and Mugwort [Artemisia vulgaris] was often used to add bitterness to beer; and Bog myrtle, also known as Sweet Gale, served the same function. Yet ale was perhaps less common in monasteries than wine was. It was said that the monks of Canterbury enjoyed wine so much that they had little room for ale, a fact that seemed to have disgusted the English peasantry [8.] But the further north a monastery was the more ale would have been used instead of wine, simply because the vine is a crop of more southerly regions. Furthermore, infirmarers used ale to administer healing herbs to the sick. It is unlikely that the ordinary lay-folk in the infirmary got their herbs in expensive wine.

Honey was also used to make some almost forgotten hybrid brews. Piment was a mixture of honey and grape juice, which would have come from the monastery vineyards. It seemed to have found favour with many monks [9.] Braggot [or braggon] was a cross between ale and mead, composed half of honey and half of malt. The great and almost forgotten delicacy was cyser, a blend between honey and apple juice, often flavoured with cinnamon. Monasteries produced much cyser and it seems to have been popular with the monks. An almost forgotten ale-strength brew was alu, honey ale. This was still brewed until the Napoleonic wars as an alternative to barley ale. While we do not know whether or not monks brewed it, they could well have done. Any drink made with honey can be flavoured with meadowsweet, which has traditionally been used to flavour mead and so might have been grown in the cellarer's garden. It certainly grows in the Sacristan's Garden at Walsham. Monks in monasteries with vineyards apparently were fond of piment, which is brewed from grape juice and honey. Infirmarers in the mediaeval period sometimes applied medicinal herbs in hippocras, which is piment with herbs and/or spices added.

The Physic Garden/herbarium

The herb garden was one of the most significant parts of the monastery, but it is the one garden that has almost ceased to exist in monastic settings. Until the present era medicine was primarily herbal and modern chemical medicines were little developed. People often grew and/or picked herbs to serve as their medicine chest. However, the rise of modern medicine, which is more successful than herbal medicine, has squeezed herbalism into the category of alternative therapies, though it has much to offer still. Monks were not dogmatic or traditionalistic about herbalism, it was the best medical technique on offer until the twentieth century and so in the modern era they have turned to modern medicine. They are not opposed to herbs, but they see no need to provide a therapeutic herb garden, as they once did for themselves and the local people. Physic gardens needed to be close to the infirmary and so would be generally within the abbey precincts if possible, or if not very near. At Shrewsbury, made famous by the fictional monk-healer Cadfael, the physic garden was in the general abbey precinct.

The herbs grown in the physic garden would have varied according to the local conditions, and some would have been more common than others.

Herbs for healing

The following plants might have grown in the infirmarer's garden.

Agrimony was used as a general tonic. The herbalist would use it in a tisane, a light tea.

Angelica was a popular digestive aid.

Arnica: Leopard's bane: This alpine plant was widely used in Europe to treat bruises and sprains, but it takes a skilled gardener to grow it. It may not have been common.

Balm: A refreshing drink was made from this herb.

Bay: While bay is used as flavouring, it was applied to wounds to cure rheumatic pains.

Betony: The monastic herbalist would use an infusion of betony to cure nervous headaches.

Bistort: Mixed with wine it was used as a remedy for diarrhoea.

Borage is said to give a peaceful sleep and be a cure for melancholy moods.

Chamomile: An herb that is known for its ability to remedy digestive complaints [it is similar to aniseed and ginger in this respect] it also has anti fungal properties and can therefore be used for fungal infections of the skin. Its leaves are taken as a tea.

Clary: The word means clear eye. It would have been used as a remedy for eye complaints, such as sties, in ointment form.

Clover can be used in an ointment for wounds and sores.

Cornflower: When eye problems were present cornflower was used as a wash to sooth tired or sore eyes.

Cumin was a famous healing herb now known to strengthen the immune system. It was ingested in food.

Dill was ingested as a remedy for digestive problems.

Elecampane: Chest problems and shortage of breath were treated with a drink of tea from this herb. We must remember that in a time when buildings were often draughty chest complaints were common.

Fennel: One of the nine sacred herbs of the Anglo-Saxons, fennel leaves and roots can be eaten. Taken orally it cures flatulence and is a laxative.

Feverfew was used, as the name suggests, as a remedy for fevers.

Foxglove: The source of the heart drug digitalis, foxglove was used to alleviate heart troubles, but if used wrongly it is deadly poisonous. Monastic healers would have kept this under strict control and administered in carefully measured, small doses.

Garlic: The herbalist's dream! It is now known to contain allicin, the antibiotic of last resort. It is rich in anti-fungal chemicals. Garlic is also good for the heart and apparently the sexual capacity, though one would not think that monks needed it for this purpose.

Germander: Fevers and digestive disorders were soothed with a tea made from Germander

Hawthorn: Now used as a remedy for hypertension, hawthorn berries were used as remedy for heart complaints.

Henbane: This herb is poisonous, but mediaeval healers used to apply it externally as an ointment to cure rheumatism, sciatica and arthritis. Under no circumstances was it ever ingested orally.

Herb Robert: The herb acquired this name because St Robert, the founder of the Cistercians, used it to cure people of the plague. Whether it was effective in any way is not known.

Houseleek was used in an ointment for skin complaints and for burns and scalds.

Hyssop was strewn on the floor of churches to prevent infectious diseases from spreading. At that time people thought that sweet smells drove away disease.

Iris: Apparently Iris can be used to make a pest deterrent.

Lavender: Persistent nervous headaches are calmed by lavender, which is to be sniffed not taken. It was known to have a calming scent.

Lettuce: Surprisingly lettuce used to be used as a soporific. Modern varieties have been bred from less soporific specimens, so this quality has been practically bred out of the species, but its soporific value was well known in ancient times.

Lovage: Plague victims were prescribed Lovage to eat, but whether it had any effect is not known.

Mallow: Sore throats were treated with mallow. Considering that people who are run down at the end of winter tend to suffer sore throats, mallow would have been a popular herb. Winter was a hard time in the mediaeval period.

Marigold: Cuts and insect bites were soothed with marigold ointment. Calendula cream [made from marigold] is still used by herbalists as a skin salve.

Marjoram was taken as a tea or tisane to alleviate colds, but it was also believed to strengthen the heart and reduce rheumatism.

Mint: Eaten it is an ideal digestive aid, but it was also used as an inhalant for sufferers from colds.

Parsley was consumed as a tonic herb and a cure for rheumatism.

Pennyroyal made an insect repellent.

Peony: Monastic herbalists grew this as a remedy for kidney ailments. It was also said to provide relief from nightmares.

Poppy: In the Middle Ages opium poppies and concoctions made from them were the main form of anaesthetic.

Purslane: A remedy for chest disorders was made from this herb.

Rose: Skin ointments were often made from roses. The hips are a valuable source of vitamin C, but the seed at their heart is an irritant and should not be taken. Syrup made from rosehips has a long history.

Rosemary: Often an infusion of rosemary mixed with wine was given as a cure for dizziness, dullness of mind or drowsiness. It seems to induce increased blood flow, which is why aroma therapists often use it to facilitate the healing of joints. Mixed into a liquid along with lavender it can be applied to injured or sore joints. [Do not take orally.]

Rue: Eyestrain, often caused by work in the scriptorium, where the manuscripts were copied, was commonly remedied by rue. In an age when spectacles were unknown, many people would have suffered painful eyes, so rue was important.

Sage: A remedy for sore throats. When mixed with goose grease it was used as a salve/balm for aches and pains.

Sorrel and milk sorrel may or may not have been grown, as they can be picked wild. They are used for dealing with bladder and urinary tract infections, along with dandelion, which can stimulate urination.

Southernwood makes a good flea repellent.

Tansy made a disinfectant.

Thistle: Fevers were treated with an infusion of thistle.

Valerian: This herb was used as a sedative.

Vervain is no longer used by herbalists, as it was thought to deter evil spirits.

Violet: This flower now used as an ornamental had several medicinal uses. Its leaves were made into a tea taken orally as a cure for constipation and gout. It was believed to cure cardiac disorders and insomnia.

Wormwood flowers were dried and scattered in wardrobes as an insect repellent.

Yarrow: This was once the only known remedy for nosebleeds. An ointment of yarrow would be used to heal wounds.

It is important to note that the monks possessed a body of herbal lore that was partly based on the accumulated observations of centuries and which was shared with herbal healers of the time; but while lore is a discipline which contained information derived from observation and tested by practice, it used non-scientific principles that most of us today would not think correct. Herbs were often cut according to phases of the moon or other heavenly considerations, such as sunrise and sunset, planetary conjunctions and so on. Recall that Shakespeare has one of Macbeth's witches taking "slips of yew slivered in the moon's eclipse" to make her evil brew. For mediaeval herbalists cutting at the time deemed appropriate according to the heavens was the norm and this practice continued well into the subsequent historical period. We may think this strange, but to understand mediaeval people we must realize that they inhabited a mental world different from the one which we inhabit today. It was not totally different, but there were elements in the mediaeval world-view which have lapsed from modern world-views, such as the beliefs mentioned above.

The Orchard, Vineyard, and the Burial Garden

Orchards and burial gardens were sometimes the same place. Apples, pears and plums were widely grown in monastic gardens. The precise varieties are not known for certain, but monks already knew the principle that fruit trees do not breed true and so practised grafting. In the Anglo-Saxon period apples, including crab apples, were pressed into a bitter liquid called verjuice, but after the Norman Conquest newer varieties came to be known. Apples from monastic orchards were commonly used for cider. Peaches were known in Britain from Anglo-Saxon times, only in the South of England, as they do not grow well further north, though the limit of the peach would vary according to the climate.

The interment of bodies in orchards has a long tradition behind it and it is a superb way of fertilizing the orchard soil. The modern green practice of green burial in woodlands is merely a return to monastic practice. In Mediterranean countries burial in vineyards was a common practice. In fact, the Vatican hill, where Saints Peter and Paul were buried, was in ancient times a vineyard outside the walls of Rome producing cheap wine for the sale to the lower classes and it was also used as a burial place for the poor. Monks merely maintained classical traditions in this respect. Though not every monastery used the orchard as a burial ground, fruit trees would have been grown in the cemetery. Cistercians even today do not use coffins. They merely wrap the body in a sheet, bury it and forget it. The theological ground for this is that the body is no longer of any use; only the soul matters; and it has now gone. Monks were generally buried without coffins and headstones, and their bodies provided much needed organic material for the orchard, an early example of recycling that our fastidious society that lives in permanent fear of mentioning death might do well to think about

Shoots out of Eden

As the Mediaeval period progressed new trees entered orchards. Cherries proved popular. The monks at Norwich had a cherry orchard known as the cherruzerd or orto censor [10]. Medlar, peach and occasionally almond grew in some monastic orchards; and mulberry slowly made its way into the list of fruits produced. Walnut, filbert and hazel nut grew in some pomeria. Records show that at Warden Abbey in 1296 that the Cistercians kept a vineyard, two orchards and a hopyard. It was there that they first bred the Warden pear [11] a variety still widely grown today. In Worcestershire pears still grow wild in old monastic sites. It appears that monks in that region enjoyed perry and so grew pear orchards.

One oft-overlooked feature of some monasteries was the impgarth or impyard. This was a nursery for young trees, which were known as imps. It is doubtful that smaller monasteries could afford the space for this nursery garden, but had to buy in stock.

Monasteries often had vineyards, but these were more common in the more southerly parts of the country. While the Romans had grown grapes as far north as Northamptonshire, in the mediaeval period the South West was the main area for English grapes. Some monastic vineyards were known in the Anglo-Saxon period. A few of the bigger monasteries seem to have had large vineyards. This was to serve the demand for communion wine, which is drunk in small portions and whose quality and alcohol strength does not need to be high; but also monk healers used to mix potions into wine and ale. Monks, anyway, were not averse to alcohol, as many monastery accounts show.

Abbot's garden/pleasure gardens

Abbots often had a private garden, as we learn from Walafrid Strabo, the abbot of Reichenau in Germany, whose writings about his private garden were widely read in the Middle Ages [12] An abbot's garden might well be a working spot, as Abbots often had to do business for kings, and a garden might be a place to meet visitors. Flowers and arbours were known in such gardens, roses being popular. Strabo wrote to the abbot of Fulda mentioning the wall that enclosed his garden, his private spot, about which he enthused greatly. It is likely that most abbots used an assistant to tend their gardens, but there were some who worked their gardens themselves, such as the abbot of Kinlos in 1500, who did much physical work in the monastery [13.]

Strabo did much of the work himself and wrote about it. He speaks of digging out the weeds with a mattock, making raised beds with wooden sides and fertilizing them with manure. The garden was a little square with one entrance. Paths went between the raised beds, though whether they were beaten earth, woodchip or gravel is unknown. Strabo would have had the strength to wield the mattock and do the heavy physical work, as he was only forty when he died in an accident; he drowned while fording a river. Many abbots reached their rank at a much later age and so may have benefited from the help of younger men.

Strabo's text is included to show the model abbot's garden presented in the literature of the time.

Key to the planting of Strabo's garden

1: Papaver: poppy
2: Lilium: lily
3: Rosa: rose
4: Rafanum: radices
5: Nepeta: catmint
6: Ambrosia: Achillea millefolium or Tanacetum vulgare: Yarrow
7: Agrimonia: agrimony
8: Vettonica: betony
9: Sclarega: Salvia sclarea
10: Costus: Chrysanthemum balsamita
11: Marrubium vulgare: White horehound
12: Absinthium: Artemisia absinthium
13: Pepones: melons
14: Cucurbita: cucumber
15: Mentha: mint
16: Abrotanum: Artemisia abrotanum
17: Salvia: Salvia officinalis
18: Anthriscus cerefolium: chervil
19: Ruta: rue
20: Apium: Celery
21: Gladiola: Iris germanica [gladioli]
22: Lybisticum: Levisticum officionale: Lovage
23: Pulegium: Mentha pulegium: pennyroyal
24: Foeniculum: Fennel
25: Entrance

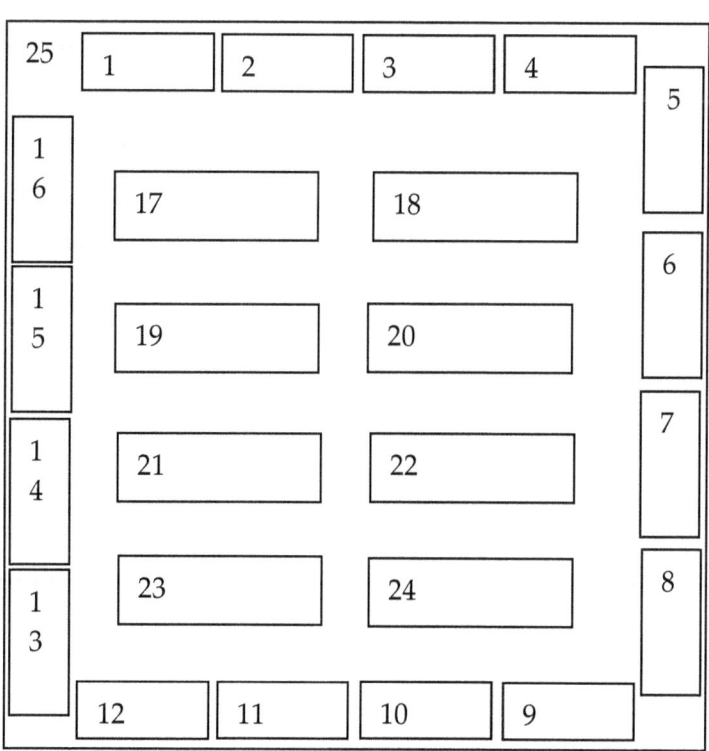

In Strabo's garden there are no bulk crops. The plants are mainly ornamentals or culinary herbs, though rose and lily were deemed to be spiritually significant, as they stood for the church, ideally beautiful as the rose and pure as the lily. Red roses symbolized Christ's blood. It is the garden planted by someone who enjoyed enough to eat and could take leisure in growing for enjoyment, meditation and sometimes taste. It was also a plot safe from predators and many invasive weeds, as it was on a lacustrine island. Strabo's main problem would have been in stopping his mint from spreading, for given a chance mint takes over the garden.

Other monks could enjoy gardens as well. In the late mediaeval period some monastery officials, such as the prior, had private gardens known as medes, tended by servants; but at Winchester there was a large three-acre pleasure garden for the monks to enjoy. These gardens were sometimes known as obedientary gardens. A herber was a small garden whose contents consisted of herbaceous perennials. It was to all extents and purposes a small leisure garden, though some of the herbs may have been used for culinary and medicinal purposes as well.

The Guesthouse Garden

While most monasteries had a guesthouse, not all would have had space for gardens. The guestenhouse, as it was called, might have had a garden of sorts, but its quality might vary from monastery to monastery, as might its size. There would have been some ornamental plantings, but it is also possible that some vegetables were grown for feeding guests.

The Green Court

This was the term given to any green area of the monastery not included in other categories, such as verges. As monasteries were quite densely packed places with religious or economic uses for most parts of them, the green court is probably not the most significant part of the monastery. It would probably contain shrubs and grassy areas.

The Monastic Fishpond

Whether fishponds were located in gardens or farms cannot be known for certain, but the fact that fishponds attract poachers would have meant that the pond would be in a protected or enclosed area, such as a garden.

Fish was an important element in the diet of mediaeval monks, when they could get it. In Lent, when Christians fasted and abstained form flesh-meat, as meat was then known, fish was very important in the diet. Furthermore, on Fridays Catholics were obliged to abstain from meat, so fish was often eaten. This practice continued into living memory, only ending in England in the late 1960s and in Ireland in 1970. Monks did not fish from the sea to any great extent, except at places such as Skellig Michael [see below] but some monasteries were fortunate to enjoy proximity to good lacustrine, inland fishing grounds, such as rivers and marshes. In general sea fishing was not very advanced during that period, mostly consisting of inshore fisheries. Inland fisheries were the main source of fish for most people. Ely, the Isle of Eels, received tithes in fish from the East Anglian fens. Glastonbury enjoyed rich fishing rights in the Somerset Levels, which were then a series of marshes and lakes often inundated by the sea.

Here the monks developed fishponds that were fed with water from the Levels. At Shrewsbury Abbey the brook that formed the monastery's southern boundary and which ran alongside the physic garden was diverted by an artificial channel to feed both the monastery fishpond and the mill. [14]

The fish generally included carp, which were introduced to England by monks. The English way of keeping fish was to have two ponds four feet deep, one of which was in use at a time. The dry one was used as an enclosure for cattle, whose dung would fertilize the ground. When it was refilled the manured ground would be ideal for the growth of water flora and fauna, on which carp feed. There was also a stew pond, into which the fish were placed a few weeks prior to being eaten. This is because carp taken from mucky water have an earthy taste. However, there were other kinds of fish eaten. Some monasteries kept a pond for pike, which are perfectly edible, but which must be kept away from the fish that you want to protect for the table, as the pike will eat them. Others kept a pool for trout.

Monastic gardeners

There were various kinds of monastic official, but only one rank is necessary to a monastery, the office of abbot. The abbot is the spiritual father to the monks and therefore is always an ordained priest, whose daily duties are primarily giving spiritual advice, conducting the services and leading the community. It is unlikely that most abbots had much to do with the administrative routine of the monastery, though Brithnoth, the first abbot of Ely, which was established by William the Conqueror, was said to have been a dedicated gardener who took serious interest in the abbey gardens. Daily management was the task of the prior, a senior monk subordinate to the abbot and responsible for administrative duties. But under him there were various roles. The gardener, known as the gardinarius or the hortulanus, was responsible to the cellarer, who was responsible for stocking the kitchens. There was good reason for this, as the products of the vegetable garden were driven by culinary need, which was determined by the cellarer. However, sacristan, responsible for the maintenance of the church and preparation of services, and the infirmarer, the monk responsible for the abbey's health, would not have been responsible to the cellarer, but more probably to the prior.

Some abbots, such as Walafrid Strabo, [see later] found time to write books about gardening. Alexander of Neckham, abbot of Cirencester, wrote a well-known horticultural treatise, De Naturis Rerum, [About Things of Nature] though it was criticized for being dependent on Middle Eastern sources and therefore not adapted to English conditions. In the seventh book of his volume of poems De Laudibus Divinae Sapientiae [Of the Praises of Divine Wisdom] he wrote about herbs. Robert Grosseteste, the saintly monk-bishop of Lincoln renowned as a fine scholar, wrote an adaptation of Palladius' De Re Rustica [About Rural Things.] This adapted Palladius' recommendations to the English climate. The Thirteenth century scholar Albertus Magnus [Albert the Great] who was something of a polymath who taught Theology to the Great Thomas Aquinas also wrote a work "De Vegetalibus" [About Vegetables.] Albert was a Dominican friar rather than a monk, but his work influenced English practice, particularly with his suggestion that plants be forced in hot houses, a practice then unknown in England, probably because it was hard to keep a place warm and well lit. Albertus wrote about the design of pleasure gardens, and he made recommendations about the maintenance of lawns. These might have had application in the cloister garth and in abbot's gardens.

The names of most of the monk-gardeners are forgotten, but occasionally a name remains, but we know of Brother John at Beaulieu, where as kitchen-gardener he enjoyed the title of curtilage keeper [15.] His accounts from the 1260s reveal that he grew beans, leeks and onions. The fact that oats and rye are included in his field of responsibility shows that he had oversight of the farming activities as well as the gardening, and the orchard was also his responsibility, judging from the fact that he produced apples for cider making. The monastery's honey production seems to have been his responsibility, as he managed to produce quite a great deal of honey and beeswax. His records mention his manure carts, which he had to mend at times. That he had permanent paths is shown by his purchase of gravel for their maintenance. Gravel paths are always a long-term feature, much more so than paths of wood chippings that can be got more cheaply than stone, but which rot down within a year or two and have to be replaced. Brother John was therefore maintaining a garden with a well-established structure. Unworldly he may have been, but he was careful with money and good at making it. His accounts show that he took in ten times what he paid his hired labourers, who probably came in on a daily basis to supplement the team of monks appointed to the gardens. We can develop a picture of a carefully maintained garden brought to maximum productivity under a skilled hortulanus.

The few records that survive from other monastic gardeners mention routine matters, such as whitewashing walls, hiring a mole catcher and ridding the cloister garth of moss. The whitewashing of walls may indicate that the Mediaevals were aware that white reflects light onto the plants, which will then benefit from the increase in light levels. This shows some gardening sophistication that belies the common image of ignorant mediaeval folk. Modern society uses the term mediaeval as a term of disapproval. People speak of mediaeval brutality, as if the twentieth century was such a gentle and civilised time; and the twenty first century has started much as the previous one left off. This usage is unfair. Mediaeval society was quite sophisticated and it was a time of steady progress that paved the way for what happened later.

Adam Vynour, hortulanus of Ely seemed to have enormous responsibilities [16.] He had to keep the accounts for the monastery and the outlying farms that it rented to tenants. Moreover, he was responsible for maintaining the gardens and their equipment and selling the surplus produce on the market. His sales included osiers [willow wood] from the monasteries outlying fenlands. Thus he seems to have had oversight not only of the abbey gardens but also of the farmlands. Some interesting points arise from his accounts. He was responsible for the maintenance of the fishpond, a fact that indicates that at other monasteries the fishpond might be seen as part of the gardens. He also had to maintain the ditches between the different monastery gardens. This is interesting, as it indicates that the abbey had several gardens serving different functions and that the boundary markers were ditches rather than walls. This practice fits into the general pattern of fenland life, a place where the land was often reclaimed from water and prone to flooding. The ditches may therefore have served not only as markers but also as drainage channels. Keeping them clear of rubbish was therefore not only a matter of tidy gardening but of preventing much of the land from waterlogging. One supposes, though, that an essentially mucky task such as clearing drainage ditches would have been performed by abbey servants, rather than monks who would have to be clean for monastic services.

That Vynour employed servants is shown in his accounts. He employed the services of a mole catcher and also paid for the cloister garth to be cleared of moss. Moles would have been a problem at Ely, as the abbey stands on a hill [once an island] above the fen. Moles cannot burrow in waterlogged land, so they would have been attracted to the dry ground on the island, at the centre of which was the cloister garth, making a mess of the monks' laund with their molehills. The numbers of monks and monastery servants that he used is not recorded.

Yet monasteries often employed external workers from the lay population. Some would have been full time employees, but others were hired for the purpose. Monasteries that had lands on which there were peasants may have taken some of their rents in labour, useful at certain times of the year. The image of the monastery as a place completely cut off from the world outside is false. While it was not a thoroughfare or a busy market, people came and went on business. Women were rare and certainly not allowed in the cloisters and sleeping areas for obvious reasons, but they were not banned from other areas of the monastery. Women would have often gone to the infirmarer for medicines.

When the torrent of anti-monastic propaganda was unleashed at the Reformation, one charge that was never levelled at the monks was mistreating their labourers. Records speak of head gardeners buying gloves and garden boots for their staff, and those gardeners who were on the permanent staff seemed to have received clothes suitable for their task, such as leggings. No one complained about underpayment of wages.

Chronological account of monastic gardens

The problem that faces any writer about monastic gardens is the dearth of records. Consider, how many allotment holders keep diaries of what they did in a day? I do not; and I know no one who does. The routine of garden work goes on, but who records its minutiae? That Brother James grew wonderful leeks one year pleased the monks who ate them, but who bothered to record the fact? The records that were kept generally failed to survive the dissolution of the monasteries. Archaeology tells us little. Stone buildings and artefacts are easier to excavate than gardens are. The destructible is destroyed, leaving nothing for posterity. Unless a name is written down or recorded in some form it leaves no trace. Thus monastery gardeners are written out of history as though they never existed. But this is so of most people, who leave at best names on a piece of paper; and their deeds and their loves are lost to posterity.

a: Before the Normans.

The beginnings of monasticism in these isles are shrouded in mist. It is possible that some early Irish sites predate St Patrick, who despite what many think, went originally on a mission to the Britons who believe in Christ in the island of Ireland, and who was adamant that he should not take the praise for other men's work in beginning the evangelization of that island. That the Celtic monks were inspired very greatly by the Desert Fathers indicates that it is probable that early Celtic monasticism took its inspiration from Egypt. There is a natural sea route from the Mediterranean via the Straits of Gibraltar to the south of Ireland, so it is likely that Christianity arrived in Ireland along it.

In Britain they begin on the Western fringe at an unspecified early date. We cannot say which monastery was the earliest monastic site, but Glastonbury could make a claim. There was certainly a monastic site at Whithorn in South West Scotland dating back to the fifth century. Certainly the pagan society that prevailed in Anglo-Saxon England had no room for monasteries and included very few Christians. Monasticism existed in Wales, although there are few if any records. It sprang up in England with the arrival of Augustine in Canterbury in 597 and independently in Northumbria, brought by Irish missionaries from the Celtic church. The two churches existed in uneasy harmony until the synod of Whitby in 667, when Roman rules prevailed. However, very little remains from the early Anglo-Saxon period.

From Ireland one site stands out almost as it was when the monks left it, Skellig Michael, where the dry stone remains of an Irish monastery nestle on a plateau beneath the summit of a 700-foot peak in the ocean west of Kerry. This is a place where Earth, sea and sky meet, on the edge of the Ocean that marked the end of the known world and the beginning of the mythical one, looking out over the sacred West, beyond which the ancient Gaels believed lay the enchanted lands of Tir nan Og, the land of eternal youth [pronounced cheer nan og, with o sounded as oh.] This was the ultimate liminal place. We can still find the remains of their monastic vegetable garden, which was constructed as a terrace on the steep slopes. It is set on the leeward side of the island, the side sheltered from the Atlantic winds, and it is walled to protect against wind and to ensure that gardeners did not fall off the cliff. In this terrace the monks heaped soil taken from the mainland, bird dung taken from the cliffs, seaweed and food remains to grow vegetables. What vegetables were grown cannot be known for certain. However, silverweed, Potentilla anserina, was a staple in the "Celtic" regions of the British Isles until the potato took over, as it is extremely nutritious and can be boiled or ground into flour to make bread. It is also a plant that tolerates salty conditions, as we can find it in coastal regions today. Leeks, onions and beans were also known in the British Isles at the time. Experiments have shown that the monks created a microclimate in the garden which fostered vegetable growth at twice the rate as on the mainland. They also had a piped water system [17]. The monks are known to have traded in seal meat feathers and eggs, swapping them for cereal and cloth. They were totally self-sufficient.

There is some dispute about the hermitage on the South Summit of the island. This was an exposed and lonely place where monks went for a retreat in total isolation. It is very hard to access on the exposed path up to it. [Visitors should not attempt this path as several have been stranded.] Some scholars think that there was a small garden up there, but no one can be sure. There is a terrace, but it is small and does not have much growing space. If there were a garden there, it would have been one of the most exposed gardens in the world, full in the blast of the Atlantic winds. But we suppose that the monks had to make use of all the space that they could, and anyway in such a small community even those spending some time in the hermitage might have had to work. There may have been other small plots on the island that we cannot yet identify.

Caldey Island was a Celtic monastic foundation linked with St Samson of Dol, and monks dwelt there from at least the sixth century until the dissolution of the monasteries. Of its horticultural traditions very little is written and there is no archaeological evidence of gardening. However, we do know that they grew herbs, as we are told in the life of St Samson that it was the custom of the abbey that herbs would be bruised and infused into the monks drink when they came in for supper. What herbs were grown is not known.

In England Jarrow has been the subject of archaeological investigation. Excavation has discovered remnants of terraces, plant holes and possible hedge lines of Saxon date. It appears that the monks were keen gardeners. Furthermore, it is likely that Jarrow's abbot, Benet Biscop, a name meaning Bishop Benedict, established a Roman garden with garden ornaments, walkways and evergreen trees. St Benet loved things Roman and made several trips to Rome. It is likely that he brought with him not only manuscripts for the library, but herbs of kinds not then known in Britain. Hyssop, rue, pennyroyal, thyme and dill possibly entered England through his work, but Jarrow would have grown some of the nine sacred herbs of the Anglo-Saxons. These are mugwort, plantain, watercress [sometimes lamb's cress] betony, chamomile nettle, crab apple and fennel [18.] The precise identity of the nine is still not agreed, and there are alternative listings. For Romans the garden was an outside room for living and working when the weather was good. It is possible then that Jarrow's most famous monk, St Bede, wrote some of the history of the English people and invented the idea of Englishness in a Roman style garden.

We look in vain for any records of gardening at Holy Island, Lindisfarne, but we find none. The monks must have grown something, but all that we can infer is that whatever they grew must have been salt tolerant and capable of surviving the winds that flay the island. The Lindisfarne Gospels, superb illuminated manuscript from the Anglo-Saxon era contains many flowers that must have been known to the monks, but we do not know whether their gardens grew them. It is possible that Lindisfarne had some lands on the mainland on which they cultivated vegetables and grew crops.

Other abbeys are mentioned in records. Worcester Abbey rose to prominence from the work of St Wulstan, one of England's greatest men, though he sadly fails to get the recognition that he deserves. He was a determined opponent of the slave trade, whose efforts managed to suppress the trade in English slaves from Bristol to the Norse slave markets in Dublin, a struggle that took him many years. His work for the poor of his diocese impressed William the Conqueror so much that he was the only Saxon to keep his episcopate after the Norman Conquest. No documentation or archaeological evidence for gardening there is present, but Wulstan established a hospital for the poor, so he must have had some kind of physic garden to supply its needs, and as herbs were administered in ale it is likely that they had brewing herbs and lands for grain. There are records mentioning a garden at Winchester during this period. At Ely in the tenth century abbot Brithnold improved the ancient monastery gardens and orchards. This abbey, rebuilt by William the Conqueror, enjoyed a reputation for vineyards, herb gardens and fishponds. The low-lying and waterlogged fens were very suitable for fishponds, as the ground is soft and wet, and the ponds are therefore easy to fill and maintain.

It is likely that the economy of a monastery reflected local economic and environmental conditions. The latter constitute a limitation on whatever can be grown on a specific site, and while monasteries are self-sustaining as far as possible, they cannot exist as though the local economy is non-existent, as most monasteries traded in some form of production.

b: After 1066

Celtic monasticism lingered on, even though many previous Celtic foundations had come under the Benedictine rule. In Scotland a fiercely ascetic extreme group known as the Culdees survived until the twelfth century, composed of dwindling communities living in isolated glens and on islets. They eked out a living by gardening and fishing. Their gardens probably consisted of lazy beds, structures commonly used in the Western Isles even today. These consist of a bed of soil heaped up and mixed with seaweed and manure, lying above soil too poor to grow much on. There are few, if any remains of these diehards of the Celtic church. There are no records of the death of the last Culdee, but he probably died a hermit, his tradition dying with him.

During the eleventh and twelfth centuries the British climate went through "the little optimum" when it was quite warm. Very quickly vineyards were established. It is certain that some vineyards were already present, as King Alfred had legislated for their protection, but better quality grapes probably entered during the Norman period. Glastonbury had a vineyard by 1086. Canterbury Cathedral, which was a monastic site, had a vineyard [vinea] and an orchard [pomerium] by the time of Thomas a Becket, both of which were outside the city walls. A document of 1165 indicates that there was a large garden and probably a herbarium [19]. The presence of piped water indicates that the gardens may have had a sophisticated irrigation system. About this time Buckfast Abbey received a charter from Henry the Second. This seems to have been a beekeeping institution. A little later King John made a grant of 12 acres of royal orchards to the priory of Lanthony, an institution dependent on Gloucester Abbey and in near proximity to it, indicative of the favour in which the English monarchy held monasteries, regarding them as a source of social stability, which, being composed of dedicated Christians, should in theory at least, be honest and prompt about their tax payments. In all probability this would have been an improvement on most of the tax paying population.

By 1283 the climate had worsened, but Winchester managed to maintain a good vineyard [20.] Vines were well established in South West England at the time, the monastery of Gloucester being particularly good for them, according to William of Malmesbury [21]. There are records of work on the prior's private garden, which was at his country house. If the prior had a country house, the abbot would have done, so we might be talking about extensive ornamental gardens associated with the monastery. We must recall that senior monks generally came from the aristocracy and so wanted to live in the manner appropriate to their rank! Records mention manuring the crab apples and tending the vines. Eight hundred stakes were purchased to support vines, and a thorn hedge was planted [22.]

Sadly, at this time came the end of Skellig Michael. The worsening climate caused huge winter storms, rendering the rock uninhabitable. The summer was as good as ever, but the severity of the winter storms meant that survival on the rock could not be guaranteed. The monks were forced to evacuate and established a site on the shore overlooking their erstwhile home. This was Ballinskellig, and it remained until the reformation hit Ireland.

There are surviving records from Glastonbury from 1334 and they make interesting reading for the insights that they give into the monastic economy [23.] The head gardener was a layman, Thomas of Keynesham, who was responsible for the orchard, vineyard, herb garden and vegetable garden, [the economically productive gardens.] Presumably the cloister garth and the Sacristan's garden were the responsibility of monks, but no records of their names remain. Strangely there seems little evidence of variety in the vegetables, certainly not enough for proper crop rotation. Onions, leeks and garlic, all members of the same family, were grown in vast quantities, with 11000 cloves of garlic produced: 3000 for seed, 2000 for the abbot's kitchen, and 6000 for the larderer [the quartermaster] for the expenses of the inn. Keynesham grew flax, linseed, and madder, a dye plant. He had three acres of apple and pear trees, as well as elm and oak. Many apples went for the making of ampelius, a form of apple juice. That there is no evidence of a balanced spread of vegetables indicates that the garden was not a home garden whose products were all eaten domestically. The monastery might have been trading produce on the markets for cash. Certainly it was the beneficiary of a rich tithing system from its lands; and the monks fished the then swampy Somerset levels, and much of the catch may well have been traded. Presumably, the monastery was moving from a system of self-sufficiency to integration with the cash economy growing at the time. Whether all monasteries followed the trend to cash economy is doubtful, as parts of Scotland, for example, predominantly used barter until the seventeenth century.

The Black Death [1348] wrought havoc with the monastic economy, as one third of England's population died. The workforce became mobile as people drifted around to find better jobs, despite laws forbidding mobility. Monasteries that relied on paid servants, such as the Cluniac foundations, therefore suffered greatly, and the order began a decline from which it never recovered. By the time of the dissolution of the monasteries there were no Cluniacs in England and the order is now extinct. Orchards seem to have suffered during this time, but a series of bad winters and cold summers was also to blame for loss of fruit. Yet the Dean of Windsor observed that many monasteries had become idle, preferring to purchase imports rather than rely on home-grown fruits [24.] We see a cash economy operating here, replacing an economic system of domestic self-sufficiency. In the early fifteenth century a series of heavy frosts did great damage to monastic vineyards. Yet the Dean observed that there were signs of a revival, for as the problems faded there were eager young monks re-establishing orchards once again and that there were plums, pears, apples, filberts and walnuts to be found [25.]

In the fifteenth century Westminster Abbey had a large infirmary garden to grow the herbs needed for medical care [26.] It was also equipped to provide food, having a fishpond and probably a rabbit warren. Later on this garden acquired a lawn for sports. This monastery garden had vineyards, orchards and bees. At Winchester there were three specialized gardens, including the leisure garden. One of these was the almoner's garden, which provided support for the monastery's charitable activities. Whether food was doled out or whether it was sold for cash used for alms is not recorded.

A minor difficulty occurred at Melrose in the early sixteenth century [27]. In defiance of the Cistercian rule against individual property some monks had been cultivating private gardens, having divided up the communal vegetable plot. The Cistercian authorities ruled against this, but the monks found a way around the edict. They simply ran a path through the middle of the plot and declared that this made it communal space again and apparently continued as before. Scotland was far from the central authority of the church, which was on the continent, and owed little allegiance outside its own borders, so the edict was never fully enforced. Then the Reformation came and people had more to concern them.

Reflections

As the mediaeval period closed Britain was a land in which the monasteries were comfortable in their place. They had lived for centuries on the same spots and felt secure for many more. The monastic gardens, orchards, vineyards and farms were old well tended and productive. Monastic affairs seemed to be running well, even though fewer entrants were joining monasteries and convents than had been the case in the early mediaeval period, probably because as society grew richer the economic security of the monastic life was relatively less attractive than it once had been. In some ways monastic garden organisation had evolved along with society, as we see that large abbeys such as Westminster and Winchester were developing more specialized gardens and were intricately involved in the economic life of the time. Not all people respected monks, as there were Lollards who in many ways were proto-Protestant, but most Britons were Catholic in sympathy if not in practice, leaving aside the undercurrent of paganism, which has always lingered on in Britain.

Probably few Britons thought that monasteries would not last until the return of Christ at the Last Judgment and even fewer bothered to think about it. Even the Lollards probably saw no real likelihood of any change. But a storm was brewing, and a cold wind would sweep away the ancient Catholic establishment and the monasteries and their gardens with it.

Dissolution

"The face of the king's servants
Turned terribly every way
And the gold of the king's servants
Grew greater everyday......
And they burnt the homes of the shaven men
That had been quaint and kind,
Till there was no bed in a monk's house,
Nor food that man could find
The inns of God where no man paid
That were the wall of the weak
The king's servants ate them all"

From the Secret People, by G.K Chesterton

The monasteries in England, Wales and Ireland fell to the King Henry's commissioners within the space of a few years, and Scotland followed with its own reformation in the 1560s. Among the last to go were the Gilbertines in 1539, their Englishness purchasing a few years for them. Truro on the Isles of Scilly, now home to a lovely garden, fell at the end of the process in 1539. The last monasteries closed in 1540. In Scotland, where the reformation took place in 1559 to 1562, the monasteries were not closed but had their lands confiscated, so they went into steep economic decline, the last one to close being Melrose, where monks are recorded as present in 1590, probably living in the ruins of a building already ravaged by the wars between England and Scotland perpetrated by Henry the Eighth. The monastery closed shortly afterwards. Some English monasteries resisted; others surrendered. Worcester, Abingdon, Westminster, Peterborough and Ely meekly yielded. The nine monks remaining at Buckfast, nestled in its Cotswold valley, could do little but surrender. Some abbots prospered from the process, for as their abbeys became Cathedrals they became bishops, e.g. Henry Holgate of Worcester, and some of their monks joined them as cathedral canons [e.g. Peterborough.] There were others such as the abbot of Abingdon and some of his monks, who took pensions. Yet there were those who resisted. Richard Whiting of Glastonbury, by all accounts a pious and holy man and diligent abbot, was hanged on Glastonbury Tor after a show trial for refusing to hand over the monastery. Some Carthusians at their London charterhouse were walled into their monastery and left to starve to death. With the monasteries went all that they had done for the English people. The schools and infirmaries, orphanages and chantries that provided homes for the aged poor were shut down. After the closure of the last Scottish abbey, monasteries ceased to exist in the British Isles and no monk gardened here for two hundred and fifty years.

The long tended monastic gardens fell into ruin, if the land was not taken by purchasers eager to grab the spoils of the dissolution and turn what were once communal gardens into private gardens for the exclusive enjoyment of one family and its guests. The gardens in the immediate environs of the abbey churches [the paradise, the sacristan's and Marian gardens] would have suffered decayed more than others, which probably became farmland or private gardens, for the abbey churches and their immediate grounds were often simply left to decay, while the abbey buildings and grounds were taken over and rebuilt as great Tudor houses. It does not take long for a garden to degenerate. Weeds soon take over, covering the ground. Self-seeded trees spring up in vegetable beds and push over stonework. The garden statuary decays and is not replaced. Soon only memories remain, the faint echoes of fading chants lingering among ancient stones, bats flitting at night in roofless churches and only birds singing in the ruined abbey churches where plainsong once soared to heaven.

One overlooked consequence of the destruction of the monasteries was the decline in honey production. Monasteries, as we saw earlier, were deeply into honey and were producing and consuming quite a lot of it, with the bees feasting on the nectar in the monastery gardens. But as the gardens were lost, so British honey production declined and honey slowly disappeared from British cuisine. Later, in the eighteenth century Britain came upon cheap sugar cane, slave produced in the West Indies, worsening the decline of honey as a major element in British apiculture. Furthermore, cyser practically disappeared from the British diet. Ever a drink made in monasteries, it did not survive their demise. Strangely Wensleydale cheese survived the dissolution. The Cistercians, who farmed sheep in Wensleydale, left the recipe to the locals when they were expelled.

Sadly history never records what happened to the gardens. We know that at Peterborough the abbey buildings fell into disrepair and they and the gardens suffered greatly from the civil war and the ensuing period of puritan rule. We hear of the quarrying of ancient churches for stone and of the despoliation of their treasures by people eager to buy goods at bargain prices, but historical books never mention the damage to cultivated land. The loss of a precious gardening culture is completely overlooked in the works of many historians. While vegetable and ornamental gardens always survive as cultural institutions, the whole idea of sacristan's and Marian gardens disappeared from British culture. While cloisters and their garths survive in some cathedrals, the monastic culture from which they sprang disappeared, and the garths became effectively ornamental lawns filling in a space whose original function was forgotten.

The monastery gardens were unimportant in the great religious and political battles of the period. There were fierce debates about ideas; there were struggles between contending politicians and ecclesiastics; and while these struggles were occurring, the handiwork of generations of monk-gardeners was being grubbed up by the new owners or given over to weeds. In the process something beautiful and good was destroyed and erased from British culture.

What became of the monasteries and gardens?

1: Heritage sites. There are several of these, though the monastery buildings are either ruined or replaced by the country houses of those who succeeded the monks. Monastery lands were sold off and the buildings left to owls, bats, looters and memories. Go to Llandyffryn in Anglesey and see the ruined priory, with the nettles flourishing in the roofless chapel behind crumbling walls. Of the monks' garden nothing remains, save the silverweed. The site is a country park, but is managed as a nature reserve. Melrose is managed by the National Trust for Scotland, which has attempted to recreate something of the abbey garden. At Glastonbury some of the buildings remain, but nothing is left of the gardens as the monks knew them. At Grey Abbey in County Down a Cistercian herb garden has been recreated, growing over fifty kinds of medicinal herbs.

Tresco Abbey, one of the last in England to fall to the King's commissioners, is now a magnificent garden run by the National Trust, which is building on the foundations left by the successors of the monks. Abbey is technically a misnomer, for it was only a priory, one step down from an abbey. In 1834 Augustus Smith, a wealthy social reformer who had purchased the island, began to develop the present gardens around the ruins of the twelfth century priory of St Nicholas. Prior to his arrival, the garden was simply abandoned. Thus there is no continuity between the monastic garden and the present gardens.

At Glastonbury some of the old buildings survive intact, though the abbey church was plundered of much of its stone and is now a ruin, one of the main looters being a Calvinist Protestant landowner who was supposed to have taken extra pleasure in despoiling the remnants of a Catholic church. Of the great productive gardens there is no trace.

2: Estates. Most abbey lands did not go to waste, as they were sold off to the highest bidder. Covent Garden [whose name derives from convent garden] was the vegetable garden of Westminster Abbey. Great estate gardens took the place of the monastic ones. Many of our great country houses were once abbeys. Beaulieu is one of them; Wenlock Priory is another. At Wenlock only one or two of the old building survive. Later owners totally restructured the gardens, leaving no trace of the monks' work. Some of these survive still in private hands. New owners always meant the destruction of old structures and the establishment of new ones. The new landowners had no use for the old monastic gardening pattern, just as they had no use for the monastery buildings. Few, if any, of the new owners were Catholics. Most accepted the established church either as Anglo-Catholics or Protestants, and Protestantism grew among the English ruling classes throughout the Tudor period. Protestants do not accept the cult of Mary, so no Marian garden could have survived. In fact honouring Mary made a person a suspected papist [an offensive and insulting term for Roman Catholics now rarely used] and liable to investigation by the ruthless Tudor security services, bent on eliminating Spanish infiltrators and sympathisers. Sacristans' gardens were no longer needed in places now no longer given over to worship and whose new owners often followed the non-ritualistic teachings of the oft-forgotten Protestant reformer Zwingli, whose works were influential among English Protestants. The Zwinglian tradition had no use for ornaments and flowers in churches, which should, in Zwingli's view, be stark and bare. The monastery gardens were replaced generally by a home garden for vegetables and a large private pleasure garden for the family that owned the estate.

3: Used as a Buddhist monastery. At Holy Island in the Clyde Estuary followers of the Dalai Lama have established a monastery. The Buddhists have a policy of respecting the Christian history of the island. They have established an interfaith conference and retreat centre and are committed to working for peace and ecological restoration. They are taking a stand against the secular West's devaluation of monastic traditions. Thirty five thousand native trees have been replanted and used to create a nature experience conducive to meditation. The Buddhists see themselves as heirs to the Celtic monks, whose love of nature and the spirit contained therein brought them to the isle. There is a women's centre from which, according to Buddhist traditions, all men are excluded. This has its own recreational gardens. It is a haven for women who have suffered abuse, a welcome survival of the old monastic healing tradition. The island is supported by the Holy Island Trust, an interfaith organization committed to peace and ecological health.

4: Surviving in Anglican use. That Worcester Abbey surrendered without resistance found it favour with King Henry, who reconstituted the abbey church as a Cathedral. This meant that the some of the grounds survived as gardens. The cloister garth remained. Over the centuries it changed in use, becoming a quadrangle in the Cathedral buildings. For some time there was a proposal to turn it into a burial site for members of the Cathedral chapter, but this was deemed inappropriate, so the proposal was abandoned in favour of a restoration project. The cloister garth was turned into an herb garden using herbs selected for historical accuracy. The modern addition is a hyssop plant, said to have been picked by General Allenby from the garden of Gethsemane, proof that even in heritage gardens there can be evolution and that gardens do not stand still. At Worcester the hospital founded by Wulstan still exists as and is known as the Commandery. Its gardens still exist but have been modified beyond recognition by the Wild family who bought the site at the Dissolution and by successive owners. It is now owned by the city of Worcester. While Westminster abbey is a national treasure, its great infirmary garden was sold off at the Reformation.

St Lawrence's, which was an old Benedictine site, was mentioned earlier on. It shares a churchyard with St Mary's Parish Church. However, St Lawrence's intends to be not a parish church, but a pilgrim church, to which people journey for emotional and spiritual healing. The trust which runs it has lovingly recreated the Sacristan's garden discussed previously. The garden is a place of prayer and emotional healing, in keeping with its monastic traditions. There are quiet garden days structured on the Benedictine routine of daily religious offices [the official round of prayers said daily by monks], teaching, shared meals and quiet times. On the first Friday of each month the first office of the day is held in the garden.

At Peterborough Cathedral the gardens were restored in the nineteenth century, primarily as an ornamental garden for the relaxation of local people. A rich herb garden runs along a cloister wall and is sometimes used by the cathedral staff when they want culinary herbs.

5: Surviving in Catholic use. Several institutions survive, reawakened after a long period of abandonment. These are Walsingham, Pluscarden, Prinknash, Buckfast and Caldey Island.

At Walsingham, a site sacred to Mary, which Catholics, Anglo-Catholics and occasionally Orthodox Christians visit on pilgrimage, the priory gardens have been restored as an ornamental garden. The gardens are primarily a woodland walk with a rich flower adornment, designed to uplift the pilgrims who come to honour Mary, who is traditionally associated with flowers, as we have seen. They are part of the spiritual experience of the shrine, for they are intended to provide the setting for peaceful reflection prayer and meditation.

Buckfast was reborn, strangely considering that it was at the Reformation one of the smallest and least significant of the monasteries. In the 1880s estate workers discovered that the foundations of the pre-reformation abbey church were still present. The Benedictines acquired the site and began to rebuild the monastery. The reconstruction was driven by the principle of restoration, as the monks are set on restoring what the Reformation destroyed. There are several components to the gardens. There is a lavender garden where the monks cultivate many varieties. The growing of this nectar-rich flower has an economic purpose, for the monastery has restored the ancient Buckfast tradition of apiculture and under the late Brother Adam, an internationally renowned authority on bees, became a centre for beekeeping. It was there that Brother Adam bred the Buckfast bee, a breed noted for its gentle character. To see bees flocking to lavender is a wonderful experience. This monastery has bucked the historical trend by restoring the physic garden, which has more than two hundred varieties of herb that would have been growing in 1539. A section for poisonous herbs that have some utility is maintained on an island in an artificial lake. The medicinal herbs are used in Buckfast tonic wine, itself a reminder of the great brewing and winemaking tradition in Catholic monasteries. [The Roman Catholic Church has never shared the Protestant tradition of teetotalism.]

The sensory garden is intended to be a spiritual place conducive to peaceful meditation. Water runs down the middle of the garden, to create a peaceful atmosphere. The garden is centred on a chamomile seat and a large Japanese maple. The seat is surrounded by a rose trellis and the garden is richly blessed with roses of several kinds. There is also an arbour designed with fruit trees, mainly apples and pears, to restore the monastic tradition of fruit growing.

Priknash, a Benedictine Foundation in the Cotswolds, was associated with the Benedictines from 1096 to the dissolution. In 1928 the monks regained the site and built a monastery. It has a magnificent deer and bird park, stocked with peacocks and other fowl, roe deer and fallow deer etc. The function of this glorious park is to create a monastic ambience and also to serve as a money earner. There is an abbey garden, which contains elements of monastic gardens. Roses are grown as decoration for the church. There is orchard and a walled home garden that produces food for the kitchens. However, the land is not ideal for fruit growing, as it is three hundred feet above sea level in the Cotswold Hills. The abbey eats some of the produce, but it also sells surplus. However, the community is suffering a manpower problem to the extent that the monks have recently decided to abandon the modern abbey and return to the older building in the abbey grounds that they inhabited when the abbey was founded and became for a short time the guesthouse, as the modern abbey is too large for them.

Pluscarden near Elgin is the only pre-reformation monastery building still in Catholic hands and serving its original purpose, being returned after a gap of two hundred and sixty one years. Originally occupied by the Vallicausians, a now extinct order combining Benedictine fraternity with Carthusian strictness, the site is now occupied by Benedictines, to whom it was donated by a Catholic landowner. While the building was a ruin, it still had some structure and was restored. In 1587 there were still one or two monks in residence, and it is possible that some monks remained until the 1590s, aided by the family of the last pre-reformation prior, who had taken control of the monastery lands [28.] As the family sold the estate in 1594 it is likely that the last monk was gone by then. The monastery began its restoration in 1948. The restoration continues apace, and there is a substantial garden. As Pluscarden trades in the products of its apiary, notably St Benet's Balm™, honey and beeswax polish, it needs a substantial flower garden to maintain its bees.

Yet the lure of islands is still strong, and some monasteries have been established on island sites. Caldey Island has been Celtic, Roman Catholic, Anglican and Roman Catholic again. Off the coast of Pembrokeshire it was a Celtic site until its community merged into the Roman Church, but it disappeared at the dissolution. In 1910 it became the home of an Anglican community, who converted to Roman Catholicism in 1913 and then sold the island to the Cistercians. The Cistercians farm the island, in keeping with their predominantly agricultural traditions, selling the dairy products such as yoghurt and making perfumes out of island flowers.

Golgotha monastery on Papa Stronsay, a small island in the Orkneys, is in something of a strange religious position. It belongs to the Transalpine Redemptorists, a strict religious order belonging to an ultra-traditional sect, the Society of St Pius the Fifth, often known as the Lefebvrites, who are now out of communion with the Roman Church because of a dispute over changes to the format of the mass. The monks have revived the Egyptian/Celtic tradition of seeking a desert. That the island is called Papa indicates that it was a monastic site and remains of a monastery from the Pictish period have been found, though it was not selected because of its monastic history. The monks make their living by farming cattle and sheep, but they grow their own potatoes and turnips. Beekeeping would be hard on such a windy place and fruit growing nigh impossible. No advanced horticulture is possible for a community, many of whom spend half the year away, ministering to traditionalist Catholics who still celebrate mass in Latin. However, there are moves to reunite this group with the Roman Catholic Church and what the monks will do then remains to be seen.

The style of horticulture/agriculture that they have adopted seems to be in keeping with the traditions of the Celtic monks, who never developed the sophisticated gardens of the Benedictines, but this is probably related to the geographical conditions of the sites where their monasteries were located. Some crops are impossible on a northern, wind-swept island, and the range of flowers that can be grown for the sacristan's garden is limited. Their situation contrasts with conditions in the lands where monasticism was born. The Benedictine tradition was the inheritor of the rich gardening traditions of Italy and the Middle East, with the sunny climate in which grapes and other fruits would grow in abundance and in which the rich variety of flowers provided nectar for the bees. Even in England, colder than the Mediterranean lands, the climate is very suitable for horticulture. On the Atlantic fringe, however, conditions are harder than in lands with a more temperate climate, so horticulture must adapt accordingly. Quite simply, less can be grown there than in more favoured lands. One of the consequences of seeking a desert is that you have opted for a place less amenable to life than the area that you have left. The horticultural practices of the monks are the product not only of religious principles, but also of the geographical factors pertaining to where their monasteries are sited.

6: New monasteries. In recent years the rule of St Basil has arrived on these shores with the coming of some members of the Orthodox

Church.[e] Orthodox monasteries are intended to be places where humans can have a foretaste of heaven. Hence they are beautiful and well ordered. They are adorned with icons, and orthodox services are glorious occasions, a glimpse of the glory that awaits the saved souls in heaven. The principle that Earth should be a foretaste of heaven extends to their gardens, which draw upon the Mediterranean traditions expressed in Benedictine gardens and which are therefore places of beauty and civility, in which wildness is tamed and cultivation flourishes. In Britain, the small orthodox monastery of St Antony and St Cuthbert, centred on an old cottage near Stiperstones in Shropshire, is designed on the principle that to sanctify the earth you must beautify it. A cloister garth has been created and vegetable beds established. A wildflower meadow has been established and extensive planting of native woodland has been done. In the woodland are shelters where worshippers can meditate. The site is designed to unite the spiritual, aesthetic and practical, a site where Earth and heaven meet.

A recent statement by the Orthodox thinker, Doctor Oikonomou, at the World Council of Churches, March 2006 expresses Orthodox thinking very effectively [29] Speaking for the alliance of Religions and Conservation on the subject of Creation and Diakonia [religious service] he stated that the transformation of the hearts and minds of a community is integrally connected with the healing of the earth. He goes on to say that the relationship between the soul and the creator and with others involves a balanced relationship with the earth. This Orthodox theology expresses itself in an attitude to monastic grounds. The lands of the monastery must be places where humans, nature and

---

[e] The Orthodox Church is the Church of Greece and parts of eastern Europe

God are in harmony. The land must be well tilled and made beautiful and useful to humans, as God intended Eden to be. The monastic garden must be a place conducive to Hesychia, the deep stillness in which the soul finds itself able to encounter and contemplate the divine. This is not necessarily total silence, although silence is highly valued in monasteries, for birdsong can never be excluded from gardens, and who would want it to be? Hesychia occurs when the natural noises happen against a background of profound silence and calm activity.

We can see here that Orthodoxy has much in common with the Benedictine tradition, as both see the need for harmony and order in society and environment. That this is so is unsurprising, as the rules of Benedict and Basil arise from the same cultural world, the Mediterranean region in the time of the later Roman Empire. This was a world in which ordered fields, orchards, vineyards and gardens were the norm. The Greek philosopher Epicurus had recommended the cultured life as one of moderate pleasure centred in a garden. While monks were not likely to follow Epicurus' views of pleasure, they certainly approved of moderation and saw the importance of the peaceful life and the gardens in which it could take place.

Reflections

> *"Every tree is known by the kind of fruits that it bears."*
> Luke 6:43-44

The spirit that is within us manifests itself in the way in which we impact on the Earth. Both capitalism and communism have poor records on this matter, and this is testimony to their flawed value systems. Many communist societies were and are filthy and ecologically exploited, though Cuba has made progress with green horticulture. Capitalism is busy extracting the maximum out of the Earth and putting the minimum back, though there are some enlightened thinkers on the right of the political spectrum. Materialism, consumerism and the greed that fuels them are busy exhausting the Earth while well-intentioned people make sacrifices to save it.

If we are to save the Earth from ecological destruction, simple technological fixes will not be sufficient. Technology is essential, but it must be used in the right spirit. Science and technology created the industry that has caused the ecological problems that we now suffer, but to blame them is unfair. They have been used by people driven by a spirit of greed and irresponsibility. Only when they are used in the right spirit will the Earth be saved from ecological doom. To discover the spirit in which we need to approach the Earth we need to study the examples of people who have lived harmoniously with the land, those who made it flourish in their care. The ancient monks are among them. Monks were not the only people who cared for the Earth in the proper spirit, other people of varying faiths and beliefs have possessed it. But the monks are good examples of the attitudes that need to be adopted if we are to avoid ecological catastrophe.

The monastic life was governed by several vows, one of which was poverty. This is not the grinding poverty of the deprived, for as we saw monks like to be well fed and comfortable. Poverty in the religious sense denotes an attitude of detachment from possessions. It allows for the use of possessions for the common and the individual good, but it regards possessions as of merely instrumental importance, while the inner life, the life of the mind and spirit, become of prime importance to them. Persons who have this attitude are not madly keen on consumption and ownership for their own sake and do not measure the value of their lives by what he owns.

The monks of all religions, Christian, Buddhist, Hindu and Jain, try to free themselves from attachment to material goods, but this attitude is not the exclusive possession of monks. Any person can adopt it. Once this non-materialistic attitude is achieved, the world can be enjoyed but will not be exploited, because non-materialistic people will give at least as much as they take, maybe more, so the ecological decline will be halted.

The Earth flourished in the monks' care because they tended it diligently, with the patience and attention to detail that so characterises the monastic spirit. They had no yearning for quick fixes or an instant profit. Monk gardeners planted trees that they would never see come into fruit, knowing that in planting them they served God and others. That was enough for them. They tended the Earth with love, seeing every flower as a symbol of the divine, enjoying the petal as well as the panorama. Committed to a non-materialistic lifestyle, they gave to the Earth as much as they took, if not more. Not all change has been progress, and we cannot say that modern attitudes to the Earth are an improvement on the attitude of the monks.

The monks used their land for economic purposes, but economics was not their highest value or only goal. Their economic activity was subordinate to their spiritual lives, in which they served a sacred reality higher than man or economics. The monks saw the world as sacred, something good that had to be respected and tended in gratitude to its creator. This attitude seems to have born fruit, for their lands were well cultivated and they turned degraded places into fertile land once again. Modern humans, who are just learning that the earth is not an inexhaustible mine for extraction of maximum profit in the minimum time, could learn much from their monastic forebears and realize that we can only care properly for the Earth when we learn that it is a sacred place to be cherished rather than a feeding trough to be consumed and respect it as such. Perhaps the most important thing that we can take from the monks is their spirit [30.]

References

1: Sacred Gardens, Martin Palmer and David Manning, Piatkus p56, 2000
2: www.gardenvisit.com
3: Sacred Gardens, p38
4: A Little History of British Gardening, Jenny Uglow, Chatto and Windus, 2004
5: John's Gospel, chapter 4, verse 14
6: www.melrose@bordernet.co.uk
7: A Little History of British Gardening, p17, 23
8: Country Wines, Mary Aylett, p59, Odham's 1953
9: Ibid 078
10: In a Monastery Garden, Reginald and Elizabeth Peplow, David and Charles 1988, p84
11: Green Enchantment, Rosetta Clarkson, Collier books, 1940, p25
12: www.uniduisberg.de/institute/CollCart/hortus/stra
13: Green Enchantment, p21
14: Cadfael Country, Rob Talbot and Robin Whiteman, pp75-80, Macdonald and Co, 1990
15: A Little History of British Gardening, Jenny Uglow, p28, Chatto and Windus, 2004
16: Ibid, p29
17: www.dioceseofkerry.ie/pages/heritage/scellig/htm
18: englishheathenism.homestead.com/nineherbsmodernenglish.html
19: In a Monastery Garden, pp140-142
20: ibid pp160-162
21: Green Enchantment
22: In a Monastery Garden p161

23: ibid pp146-147
24: Ibid pp81-82
25: Ibid p82
26: Ibid p160
27: www.Melrose@nbordernet.co.uk
28: www.pluscardenabbey.org
29: www.arcworld.org/news.asp?pageID=117
30: Jerusalem Bible, Darton, Longman and Todd, 1985

Useful address:
The St Lawrence Trust
The Street
South Walsham
NR13 6DQ

St Lawrence Trust has a website which will provide information about opening times and where to stay in the vicinity. Accommodation is available near the site.

www.ingramcontent.com/pod-product-compliance
Lightning Source LLC
Chambersburg PA
CBHW070935160426
43193CB00011B/1692